SYMI
A PRACTICAL
GUIDE

By

Clive Davies

Updated for 2024

For Sindy, The 'Queen of Symi'

TABLE OF CONTENTS

INTRODUCTION

I t is hard to characterise why Symi is so special amongst the Greek islands, and why visitors return to this neo-classical Aegean gem year after year, often more than once.

It certainly captures a special place in many people's hearts. It seems to put a spell on them. Perhaps it's the reliability of the summer weather which is guaranteed to be warm and sunny for months on end. Or perhaps it's the crystal-clear sea and the quirky beaches and hidden coves. Perhaps it's the harbour, buzzing with activity or the warmth and generosity of Symiots themselves.

Perhaps it's the glorious setting and the many different colours of the houses cascading down to the sea and reflecting in the perfect harbour. Perhaps it's because, being relatively small, there is only so much to see, and more time can be devoted to the art of relaxing, swimming, eating, drinking and generally having a good time.

Perhaps it's the island's history, with its ups and downs, its waves of conquerors and the legacy they have left on this barren lump of rock.

It may be some of these things, all of these things, or none of them. Whatever it is will probably remain an enigma. You will have to go and look for yourself and see if you too fall under the island's magical spell.

Nimos

Symi Bay

Agia Marina

Nimborio

Nos

Toli Bay

St Nicholas

Roman Mosaic

Pontikokastro

St Emilianos

Pedi Bay

St Michael Roukouniotes

St George

St Michael Kokkimides

Wine Presses

War Memorial

Nanou Bay

Meghalos Sotiris

St Michael Kourkouniotis

Wine Presses

Marathounda

Panormitis

Monastery St Michael Panormitis

Symi Island

N
W — E
S

Seskli

GETTING THERE

One of the attractions of Symi is that it takes a bit of an effort to get there. You can't just fly in and flop on a sun-lounger 30 minutes later. This has its benefits as it tends to limit the amount of tourism to manageable numbers.

Travelling to Symi for independent travellers requires an element of planning, although actually booking the various stages of the journey is fairly straightforward.

Some people choose to book via a tour operator, particularly for their first visit, and then all of the stages of the journey are arranged for you.

The most popular and easiest journey is to fly into Rhodes and then take a ferry across to Symi. It is also possible to fly into Kos and take the ferry from there, although frequencies are fewer, and the journey time is longer.

An alternative is to fly to Athens (a great destination in its own right for a few days) and then either fly on to Rhodes or take the ferry from Athens Piraeus port to Symi overnight.

There is an excellent travel blog by Andy Ward, which is updated regularly with the latest news on ferries to Symi and on flights to Rhodes and Kos from a number of countries. This can be found at http://www.andyward.me.uk/symiblog/

FLIGHTS

Scheduled and charter flights operate from many cities in Europe to Rhodes during the Summer season (May to October).

From the UK there are daily flights in the Summer, with the highest frequency normally on Wednesdays and Saturdays. Scheduled operators include Ryanair, easyJet, Jet 2 and British Airways. Olympic Air /Aegean Airlines also fly from Athens to Rhodes.

Rhodes island is a big destination for tour operators from all over Europe and some of these, including TUI, sell seat-only tickets as well. A good site for comparing seat prices, including tour operator seats is http://www.cheapflights.co.uk

Although many tour operators serve Rhodes, few serve Symi itself. An exception is Olympic Holidays http://www.olympicholidays.com which has served the island for many years and offers a good selection of flights and accommodation. Sunvil also offers a more limited range of holidays to Symi from the UK (https://www.sunvil.co.uk/). Some European tour operators also serve the island from Germany and the Netherlands, in particular Attika Reisen (https://www.attika.de/).

FERRIES

The main ferry companies currently serving Symi are Sebeco Lines, Dodekanisos Seaways and Blue Star Ferries. They can be found at https://www.sebeco.gr/en/, http://www.12ne.gr/en/ and https://www.bluestarferries.com/en-gb respectively.

Other operators tend to come and go. Recently SAOS ferries (www.saos.gr) and Seadreams (https://www.seadreams.gr/en/) have also been regularly serving the island so be sure to check these operators too.

A good site on which to compare all ferries operating on a particular day is ferryhopper.com, which also has a useful app through which it is also possible to make bookings (https://www.ferryhopper.com/en/)

Ferry schedules change every year but are generally bookable a few months before the summer season begins.

Sebeco Lines serves Symi a number of times daily in the summer period. In 2023 the company had two boats operating the route with a very good frequency of up to five services per day each way between Symi and Rhodes. The journey time is about

90 minutes. Tickets are bookable via the website and no longer have to be collected prior to boarding. The availability of ferries throughout the day means it is often possible to connect straight through to Symi in a single day with morning flights from northern Europe.

Dodekanisos Seaways serves many of the Dodecanese islands with Symi being the first stop on the northbound itinerary from Rhodes (and the penultimate stop on the way back). The operation is efficient and uses a combination of modern fast catamarans and a larger ship, the Panagia Skiadini.

In 2023, Symi saw a reduced service from Dodekanisos but still benefitted from several weekly services. Typically, Dodekanisos ferries leave Rhodes at 08:30 and/or 09:30 and the journey time to Symi is between 50 and 90 minutes depending on the ship. Be aware that the Panagia Skiadini travels via Panormitis on some days of the week, lengthening the journey time. The return ferries typically depart Symi at 16:30 or 17:30 making it possible to connect with later outbound flights from Rhodes.

Blue Star Ferries also serves Rhodes and Symi two to three times per week on the Piraeus-Symi-Rhodes-Symi-Piraeus route. Again, schedules change but typically departures from Piraeus (Athens) are on a Tuesday and Thursday afternoon (and more recently Sunday also) arriving early morning in Symi on the following day en-route to Rhodes.

The journey time between Athens and Symi is approximately 16 hours, although faster ships coming into service are reducing this. The ship stops at several other islands, including Kos, on the way. Overnight cabins are available. In the return direction, the operation connects Rhodes with Symi, normally on a Monday, Wednesday and Friday evening en-route back to Athens.

In 2023, the **SAOS ferry** 'Stavros' served Symi on an outbound schedule from Rhodes up to Kalymnos and Astypalea twice a week (via Tilos, Nisyros and Kos), on Monday and Thursday and back to Rhodes (via Symi) on a Tuesday and Friday, continuing on to Kastellorizo and Halki respectively. This provided a direct connection between Symi and these other islands.

In addition, the Seadreams catamaran 'King Saron' operated daily (sometimes up to 3 services each way per day) between Rhodes and Symi.

When travelling between Rhodes and Symi, there are three harbours for Rhodes town (see map below). The Dodekanisos fast ferries, as well as Sebeco, leave from Kolona harbour whilst the larger Dodekanisos ship (the Panagia Skiadini), the Blue Star ferries and the SAOS ferry Stavros leave from Akandia Harbour, slightly further to the south. The Sea Dreams King Saron departs from the Tourist Port.

Reservations made online (take a printout with you) can be exchanged for paper tickets at booths adjacent to the ship's departure points, although Dodekanisos, Blue Star and Sebeco now also accept electronic/pre-printed tickets.

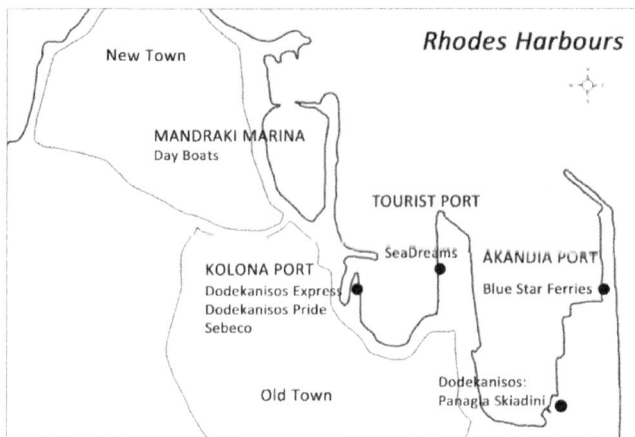

Rhodes Harbours

New Town

MANDRAKI MARINA
Day Boats

TOURIST PORT

SeaDreams

KOLONA PORT
Dodekanisos Express
Dodekanisos Pride
Sebeco

AKANDIA PORT
Blue Star Ferries

Old Town

Dodekanisos:
Panagia Skiadini

When arriving in Symi, Blue Star ferries use the new commercial quay, which is the furthest quay from Yialos (at the very far end of the south quay). Dodekanisos ferries and Seadreams continue to dock at, or close to, the Clock Tower (north quay).

Sebeco ferries dock on the south quay, adjacent to the bus stop. The SAOS ferries and the Dodekanisos Panagia Skiadini are supposed to use the new commercial quay but often use the clock tower. If you require further information, then contact the local port agency Symi Tours on +30 22460 71307. Be sure to also follow them on social media for ferry updates.

Be aware that in bad weather, particularly if wind speeds increase, ferries can be cancelled at short notice. In these circumstances, the Blue Star ferries tend to be the most reliable as they are large ships less affected by the weather. The catamarans and the Sebeco are lighter ships which are more prone to delays and cancellation. If you suffer from seasickness, you may find the larger ships to be more stable in high winds and rough seas. Depending on the weather forecast, it is often worth considering heading back to Rhodes the day before your flight to be on the safe side.

Up to date information on flights from various European countries to Rhodes and Kos, as well as the latest ferry schedules can be found on Andy Ward's excellent blog at http://www.andyward.me.uk/symiblog/

TRANSFERS

The easiest way to transfer between the airport in Rhodes and the ferry ports is by taxi. There is a fixed fare between the airport and Rhodes Town (around €29.00 at time of writing). If staying in Rhodes Town, the taxi from the town to the harbour is around €10.00 or less. There is also a bus connection between the airport and Rhodes Town, departing just outside the terminal building. Journey time is about 40 minutes and the fare is around €3.00.

DAY TRIPS FROM RHODES

If you are staying on Rhodes, there are day trip excursions to Symi during the summer season. This is an ideal way to get an impression of the island and to decide whether you might like to holiday there in the future. There are a number of operators, and excursions are bookable either through agents on Rhodes or online. These are good value trips, typically costing around €40 per person and include the return fare to Symi and a guide to show you the main sites around the harbour at Yialos. Some trips also stop at Panormitis or stop in one of Symi's bays for swimming. One of the largest operators is Sea Dreams and excursions are bookable online via its website. https://tours.seadreams.gr/home

ISLAND HOPPING

As Symi is the first stop on the ferries travelling northbound from Rhodes, it is possible to combine a visit to Symi with other Dodecanese islands, without necessarily having to go back to Rhodes (although doing so does provide a greater choice of destinations).

The Dodekanisos ferries go north from Symi calling at Kos, Kalymnos, Leros, Lipsi and Patmos, whereas the Blue Star ferries vary depending on day of the week – for example, the Friday ferry calls at Tilos, Nisyros, Kos, Kalymnos, Lipsi and Patmos on its way to Piraeus.

The SAOS ferry also links Symi directly to Halki, Tilos and Nisyros. Thus, by combining ferries, a number of onward destinations are available (as well as return routes to Rhodes).

WHEN TO GO

Symi's location means it generally benefits from long hot summers, although winters can be surprisingly wet and cool.

The main season for visiting is May to October with the peak months of July and August being the hottest, when temperatures can easily reach in excess of 35 degrees Centigrade and rainfall is virtually non-existent. This is *Kalokairi*, the Greek for Summer, but which also translates as 'The good time'.

During summer, the dry *Meltemi* wind often blows from the north, providing some distraction from the searing heat. However, due to the fact that Symi is largely a fairly barren rock with little vegetation, the island tends to act as a heat sink and temperatures tend to be considerably hotter than those in Rhodes.

Bear in mind also that the temperatures that appear when you research 'Symi weather' tend to be those for Rhodes, sometimes with an 'adjustment' for Symi. These can be somewhat inaccurate as there is no physical weather station on Symi itself.

For those who aren't so fond of the heat, May, early June, September and early October offer some respite (daytime mid to high 20s Centigrade) and are popular months with hikers.

Taxi boats to the island's beaches operate from the beginning of June to mid-October, depending on the weather, and good ferry schedules operate well into October and up to the Panormitis festival on 8th November, before reducing for the winter months.

Winter temperatures can vary widely from 7-15 degrees Centigrade and have been known on occasion to drop below freezing. There is normally significant rainfall between November and March with the most falling in January & February. In recent years the climate appears to have changed slightly with October being generally more reliable for sunshine than April.

Winter can definitely bring some nasty weather. On 13th November 2017, Symi was hit by an unusually persistent storm, 'Storm Eurydice', which deposited a massive amount of rain on the island. This caused extensive damage as it ran off the mountain and into Yialos, depositing a substantial amount of rock and mud in the harbour. Ancient steps in Stavros Square in the village were washed away, new ravines have opened up and a number of cars and possessions were washed into the harbour. The resilient Symiots, with help from Rhodes, and donations from regular visitors, quickly repaired the damage in time for the Summer season in 2018.

Symi Harbour

A BRIEF HISTORY

The casual visitor to Symi may wonder who built all the pastel coloured houses and why there are so many on what appears to be largely a barren rock. Well, for a relatively small island, Symi has quite a story to tell!

There are a number of different (and sometimes conflicting) stories within the Greek Myths on Symi and how it came to be given its name. One story involves the mythological figure of Glaucus, a fisherman and boat-builder, who was originally mortal, but became immortal after eating a local herb and was transformed into a sea god. The author Athenaeus, citing the Greek historian Mnaseas, tells us that on his travels back from Asia, Glaucus abducted Syme, the daughter of King Ialysos of Rhodes, brought her to the island and bestowed her name upon it. Another myth suggests that Zeus, the sky god, turned Prometheus (son of Iapetos, a name used on the island to this day) into a monkey ('Simis' in ancient Greek), where he was kept until his death.

As well as 'Symi', the island has also been known by a number of other names over time, including 'Metapontis', which is a name still used on the island, and 'Aigli'.

The recorded history begins with references to Symi by Homer in his famous poem 'the Iliad', believed to have been written in the 8th Century BC and set during the Trojan War. In Book II (lines 671-675), when Homer is cataloguing the ships on the Greek side of the battle, he records that (King) "Nireus from Syme brought three fine ships", as well as describing him as "One of the most handsome of all Greeks". It is clear then that Symi was already engaged in shipbuilding and played her part in defeating the Trojans, although it is also mentioned that Nireus was tragically killed at some point during the battle.

The island's location resulted in a number of different early ethnic groups either visiting or attempting to settle throughout history, including the Carians from south west Anatolia (Turkey), the Dorians, who also settled in Rhodes, the Peloponnese and Crete, and early Greek 'Pelasgian' peoples.

In Roman and Byzantine times, the island was closely affiliated with Rhodes and was known as a supplier to the empire of good, fast ships and excellent seafarers. In fact, the island was one of the Byzantine naval bases charged with the task of controlling the eastern Aegean Sea and the Mediterranean as far away as Syria. Although little remains of this period today, there are clues, including a mosaic, probably from a Roman villa of the time, located in Nimborio.

The Kastro

In 1309, the island was conquered and occupied by the Knights Hospitaller of St John at the same time as they conquered Byzantine Rhodes to replace Cyprus as their home territory. The Knights enhanced the fortress Kastro on Symi, as well as building the magnificent Palace of the Grand Master of the Knights on Rhodes.

Despite regular attacks from Turks, Symi remained under control of the Knights until 1522 and during this time the island capitalised on its strategic location and prospered by continuing to supply fast ships to the Knights for their growing commerce and trade.

In 1522, the Ottoman Empire defeated the Knights in both Rhodes and Symi. However, the canny Symiots, who had always maintained close links with the Turks, sent high quality sponges and Symi bread to Sultan Suleiman the Magnificent as an offering. In return for agreeing to Ottoman 'rule', and for regularly supplying the Sultan with such goods, Symi was granted a number of important privileges, under a formal agreement or *Firman* under Islamic law. These privileges, which were instrumental in securing the island's future prosperity, included: -

❖ A high degree of autonomy including the right to self-maintain the fort (Kastro) and island's defences,

❖ Freedom from Ottoman taxes apart from an annual *Maktou* (a token payment) and a supply of sponges to the Sultan's harem,

❖ The right for the island to retain its own religion (there are no mosques on Symi).

❖ The right to cultivate land on the Turkish mainland,

❖ The sole and exclusive right to fish for sponges throughout the seas of the Ottoman Empire.

It was this last privilege that really kick-started the prosperity of the island, given the growing demand for natural sponges at that time. This resulted in Symiots becoming more and more skilled and adventurous at sponge diving and building larger and larger boats accordingly. Symi's sponge divers travelled as far as North Africa and even as far as the Canary Islands.

During the 16th and 17th centuries, Symiot ships gained the right to fly the flag of St Mark as a protection from pirates by paying a small tax to Crete, which was then ruled from Venice.

The period between the granting of the privileges in 1522 right up to the early 1900s was the period of maximum prosperity for the island.

The first two centuries of Ottoman rule saw little in the way of art being produced on the island, but from around 1700, religious painting flourished and many fine examples remain to this day.

It was in the mid to late 19th Century when sponge diving reached its peak that many of the pastel-coloured houses were constructed in the neoclassical style, some with beautifully painted ceilings. The 'Kali Strata' was also constructed at this time and the island's population had soared to around 22,000 people by 1900.

The island became a trade hub and there were at least 30 ship-owning merchant families on the island, a tannery, a slaughterhouse, theatre, library, town hall, infirmary and schools to serve the growing population. Symi had become a very rich island.

Following the Greek War of Independence (1821-1829), Symi was left out of the resulting Greek State, and remained under Ottoman rule until the Dodecanese Federation declared independence in 1912.

By this time, the sponge diving industry was declining and Symiots were emigrating to seek new opportunities in Australia, the United States, France and other parts of Europe. The population declined rapidly and today the resident population of the island is no more than 2,500 people.

In 1912 the Islands were occupied by Italy before being formally ceded to that country in 1923. Because of this the island retains an Italian flavour and many of today's tourists still come from the country.

In 1939, when World War II broke out, the Dodecanese islands were still occupied by Italy, but later in the war German troops arrived on the island. Allied forces mounted a number of attacks during the German occupation and there was significant combat on the island. At one point the German positions were attacked by allied aircraft and a number of bombs were dropped, destroying some houses.

In October 1943 an allied Special Boat Squadron operating in the Dodecanese learnt that Kos had been taken by German forces and docked in Symi, together with members of 74 Squadron RAF who were also originally bound for Kos by ship. On 6th October 1943, German forces arrived on Symi from Rhodes, landing at Pedi and making their way up into the village. A fierce battle duly ensued, known as the 'Battle of Simi'. With German forces being supported by Stuka bombers, the allied forces eventually retreated to Kastellorizo.

On 13th July 1944, according to historian David Heffernan, a joint force consisting of 100 men from the Royal Navy Special Boat Squadron (SBS) and 224 men from the Greek Sacred Band (the Greek special forces unit), approached Symi under the cover of darkness. The following day they surprised the Italian and German forces on the island with an attack on the harbour, the Kastro and further inland. They had effectively secured the island but as Luftwaffe aircraft began to attack they decided to withdraw, sinking a number of German military vessels as they retreated. The raid, known as 'Operation Tenement,' had been a success. Although sadly a handful of SBS and Sacred Band men were killed, 21 German troops were also killed and 150 were captured.

There followed a number of similar raids on German occupied islands by the SBS and Sacred Band across the Aegean islands which then expanded to the Peloponnese and Albania, thereby holding down German forces and preventing them from joining the Western and Eastern fronts.

At the end of the War, the occupying German forces are believed to have ignited their remaining ammunition in buildings just below the Church of the Assumption of the Virgin Mary (the Megali Panagia), destroying the church, many fine houses and causing significant damage to the whole of the Kastro site. Consequently, many ruins remain around the Kastro to this day.

Importantly, the German surrender of the Dodecanese Islands was formally accepted from German General Otto Wagener by British forces at the Town Hall in Symi (now LOS restaurant and gallery) on 8th May 1945. The British then briefly occupied Symi until it was handed back to Greece in 1948.

German Forces Surrender on the 8th May 1945 in the (then) Town Hall

(Picture credit unknown but from ww2helmets.com)

Symi Town Hall (now LOS Restaurant and Bar)

As it is these two industries that define what Symi has become today, they deserve a little closer examination.

Since the earliest times, Symi was known and respected for its boatbuilding prowess and for its seafaring expertise. The proximity to Turkey, and the ability to easily source timber from there, led to Symi developing state of the art shipbuilding skills. Boats were built at the mouth of the harbour in Yialos (now the village square) and at Harani (where they are still serviced today).

Harani Boatyard

The island constructed the famous *Symi Skiffs*, which were known to be the fastest boats in the Aegean, prized by the Ottomans (and the Knights before them) and used to carry their mail. Symi also produced 2 and 3 masted schooners, caiques for the sponge diving industry and other craft for both local ship owners and for clients on other islands. Many of the wooden ships built in Turkey to this day are believed to be based on Symi designs. In the 19th Century, Symi's commercial fleet numbered over 200 vessels. However, it was the invention of the steam ship that finally put an end to Symi's shipbuilding trade.

Symi and its surrounding islands were once synonymous with natural sponges which grew prodigiously in the clean and fertile Aegean waters. References to sponges go back as far as those contained in at least three chapters of Homer's Odyssey (8th Century BC) and even Glaucus was believed to have been one of the first divers, but it was during the Ottoman times that they came to be prized so highly.

The earliest records of sponge diving date back to the 15th Century when they were harvested by skin-diving with a *trident* but, as demand increased, greater risks were taken. Divers began descending from the boats with a heavy stone against their chests to speed their descent to the seabed. These stones were prized and handed down from generation to generation, but the divers still relied on holding their breath and so harvesting was repetitive and slow and confined to the shallower waters. This was the time of the legendary Symi diver Stathis Hatzis, who is commemorated with a statue on the quay in Yialos.

In 1863, a local man, Fotis Mastorides introduced the diving suit to Symi (known as 'scafandro' in Greek), probably a version of Augustus Siebe's enclosed contraption invented in 1819. This suit, which was fed air from the surface, meant that divers could stay underwater for long periods, descend to greater depths and harvest many thousands of sponges. It was actually demonstrated by his wife (Evgenia), who was the first person to dive with the suit in Symi harbour in 1863. She demonstrated the suit (while pregnant) in order to convince the otherwise skeptical sponge divers to use it rather than diving naked and holding their breath. A statue on the main quay commemorates her.

This invention triggered the golden age for Symi (1870-1910) and it became one of the wealthiest ports in the Mediterranean with the Captains of the diving boats earning a fortune. The population expanded rapidly and trade with Turkey increased to service the island. Many of the neoclassical houses and other buildings were constructed at this time.

Following the industrial revolution, the demand for sponges became insatiable from all round the world. Bigger dive boats were built, accommodating up to 40 divers, but soon demand began to outstrip supply and the divers started to go deeper and deeper. At that time, there was no knowledge of the risks to the body from diving, and particularly the effects of nitrogen narcosis when diving at depth.

Consequently, many divers strayed too deep or stayed at depth for too long, becoming disorientated and unable to signal to the surface. Without a signal from below, crews hauled the divers up too rapidly, resulting the affliction known as *the bends*, which caused vomiting, nerve damage, paralysis and all too often, death.

By this time, the diving boats, having exhausted the supply of sponges around the Dodecanese islands, would travel as far as the north coast of Africa to fish. They would leave Symi in the spring and not return until autumn, and when they did return there were fewer divers. Too many of the young men of Symi died or were crippled for the rest of their lives.

Some divers left Symi to join the newly formed sponge diving industry in Tarpon Springs, in the United States, where the diving was less demanding than that in the Mediterranean.

Sponges on Display next to Dinos Sponge Centre

By 1910, the physical toll of diving, and the long periods of absence from family and friends resulted in Symiots recruiting divers from other islands, particularly Kalymnos, but by 1920 competition from artificial sponges and migration from the island to Australia, America and other parts of Europe resulted in the decline and eventual death of the sponge diving industry on Symi.

So, sponge diving has left us with the beautiful harbour we see today and the myriad of neoclassical buildings, but we must remember the price that many paid for the island's period of prosperity.

The sponges available today are not from Symi waters but they make excellent gifts which are light to pack and which will remind you of the island's illustrious past.

ARCHITECTURE

Although there are many older buildings on Symi, the majority of the houses are believed to date from the period of the island's maximum prosperity, when the sponge-diving industry was at its height.

Symi Architecture

Although similar architecture is seen on some other islands, building on Symi was clearly influenced by the neo-classical style (which is an 18th Century style derived from buildings of classic antiquity and the interpretations of these by Andrea Palladio and others in the 16th Century). The vernacular architectural style on Symi can probably therefore best be described as 'Aegean with neo-classical elements', although the terms *Venetian* and *Italianate* terms are also used.

This style was very much in vogue in the mid-19th Century when Greece was ruled by the Bavarian King Otto. During this time the capital was moved from Nafplion to
Athens and many important buildings in the new capital (and old) were constructed in this style (including the University of Athens and the Old Parliament Building).

Whilst avoiding Palladian columns (although some have pilasters), Symi houses tend to be geometric and two or three storey at the front, often with fewer storeys at the rear due to the sloping terrain. Typically, they will have tiled roofs, triangular pediments, symmetrical windows (shuttered) and doors and have one or more balconies with iron railings.

Interior rooms have high ceilings which are sometimes intricately and ornately painted (many survive to this day) and wooden floors. Many also have cisterns cut into the rock below to store water and some have *mousandra* lofts or elevated sleeping platforms, accessible by very steep steps or a ladder.

Today, there is a wide palette of colours, although these have to be approved by the municipal authorities as the buildings have ministerial 'historical location' protection. Traditionally the main colours were ochre, brown, salmon pink and red as these absorbed the heat better in winter, as well as blue, but more recently, with the advent of new synthetic paint technology, other colours have supplemented the palette. If you walk around up in Chorio, you can still see remnants of the much richer colours that were originally used on some of the ruins and deserted properties.

Perhaps the most interesting architectural element on Symi is the triangular pediment and more specifically the use of the *bull's eye* or *oculus* central feature. It is thought that these features were originally vents, used to let out the hot air and to cool the loft space below the roof and perhaps also to act as a pressure equaliser during strong winds. Today, many of these are purely ornamental, having been filled in and no longer usable as vents. They are a lovely feature and the variety of the designs is intriguing. Be sure to look up as you walk around – you may spot faces, crosses, stars, crests, whole figures and many other quirky designs as well as those that retain their original functional design. Two such oculi are featured on the cover of this book!

ORIENTATION

S ymi is a relatively small island (around 67 square kilometres) which lies in the Aegean Sea about 20 kilometres north west of Rhodes (approx 45km from Rhodes Town to Yialos by ferry) and about 17 kilometres south east of Datça in Turkey.

Dodecanese Islands

Agathonisi

Patmos

Lipsi

Leros

Turkey

Kalymnos

Kos

Astypalea

Nisyros

Symi

Tilos

Rhodes

Halki

Karpathos

Symi is part of the Dodecanese chain of islands which also includes Kos, Patmos, Rhodes, Tilos, Nisyros, Chalki and Kastellorizo. Looking at a map it appears to be ensnared by the Turkish Datça and Bozburun peninsulas. In fact, the island is closer to Turkey than it is to other parts of Greece, being only some 7km from the Turkish mainland at its closest point across the Dorian Channel.

As well as the main island, the geographical area of Symi also includes the smaller islands of Nimos to the north and Seskli to the south. There are also a number of much smaller islets close to the main island.

Few people will forget their first sight of Symi as the ferry pulls round the headland to reveal the fairy tale vista of one of the most beautiful harbours in Greece. Like a wedding cake with the Kastro presiding over a scattering of pastel-coloured neoclassical and Italianate villas and houses cascading down to the sea.

Such is the scramble for this view that it is best to bag a spot at the front of the ferry early on or risk the stampede as the ship approaches the harbour.

Conveniently, this view contains the two main areas of population on the Island. Sprawling over the top of the hill and over to Pedi beyond is **Chorio**, also known as 'Ano Symi' or 'the Village' and, at the bottom of the hill, around the harbor, is **Yialos,** also known as 'Gialos' or 'the Harbour'. Above the human settlements towers the mighty Vigla, the highest 'mountain' on Symi at 616 metres above sea level.

These two areas have completely different characters. The harbour area is commercial and buzzing with boats coming and going, ferries loading and unloading, a never-ending stream of vehicles going to and fro somehow dodging locals and visitors, people shopping, eating and drinking and noise!

Up in the village things couldn't be more different. Here it is quiet and languid with only the occasional tourists making it up the 400 odd steps of the Kali Strata Grand Avenue or taking the bus along the new road which connects the two settlements. It's a wonderful place to walk around, getting lost in the many lanes and ruins which surround the Kastro.

The only other settlements of any size are the sleepy villages of Pedi and Nimborio and the monastery site at Panormitis.

View from the Kastro

YIALOS

Yialos is the busy hub of the island, where boats and ferries come and go and where everyone seems to be constantly on the move. Each day in summer, several day trip boats visit from Rhodes, adding to the mayhem, but by late afternoon they have returned, handing the harbour back to those staying on the island and visiting yachts.

The harbour area consists of the south quay, north quay and the mid quay between them. Along the **South Quay** are a number of shops, tavernas and restaurants, as well as the bus stop and the taxi rank.

Towards the 'town end' of the south quay (from the bus stop) are **Pantelis Restaurant**, the **Porte Café**, **Olive Wood** giftshop, **Jimmy's Moto Rentals**, **Meet the Meat/To Spitiko Taverna** and **Haris Taverna**. Continuing towards town are the taxi rank, **Lakis Travel**, a **pharmacy**, the **Nikolas Patisserie**, the **Fotaras Café** and slightly further along the **L'Alegrito Bar**, the **Mediterraneo Bar** and the **Iliaxtida** boutique. In the lanes behind the south quay are restaurants including the **Trata** Trawler and **Bella Napoli** and hotels including the **Old Markets** and **Thea**.

Going out of town, beyond the bus stop towards Pitini, the area is mainly residential, apart from **Yachta** restaurant (above the gym) and the petrol filling station which is at the junction where the road starts to climb out of the harbour and up to Chorio. Beyond the filling station, the commercial quay has recently been opened for larger ships visiting the island. All Blue Star ferries now use this new quay and there is the combined Blue Star ticket office/**Café Rementzo** nearby which is incredibly welcome when arriving early in the morning before the rest of Symi wakes up.

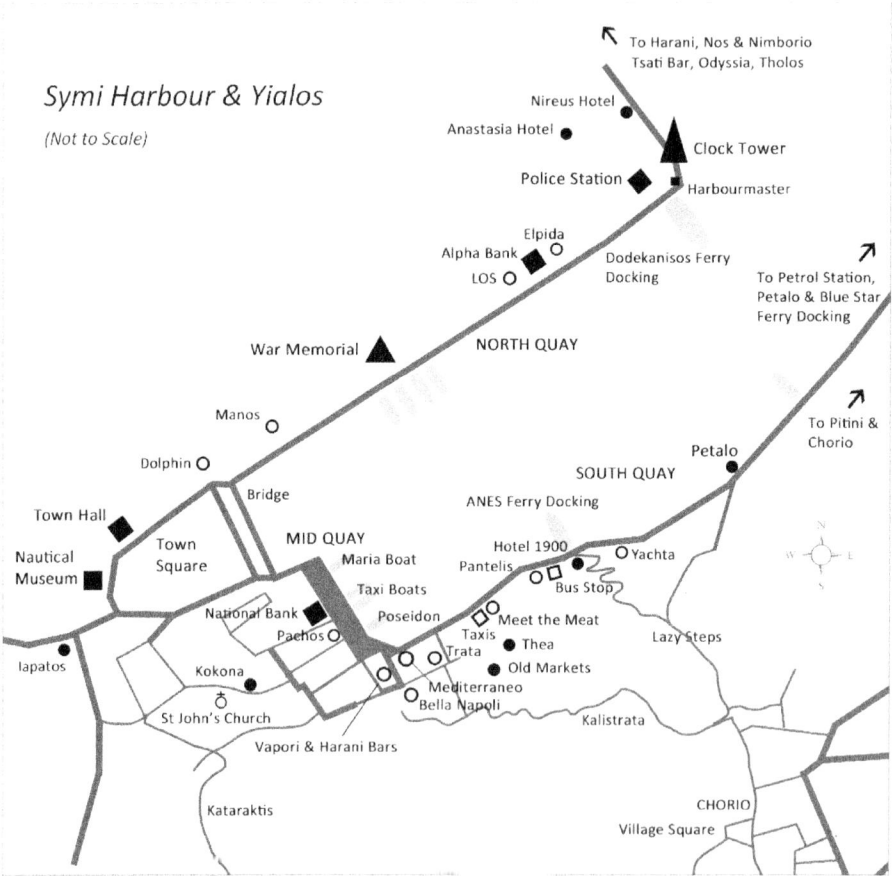

Symi Harbour & Yialos
(Not to Scale)

To Harani, Nos & Nimborio
Tsati Bar, Odyssia, Tholos

Nireus Hotel
Anastasia Hotel
Clock Tower
Police Station
Harbourmaster

Elpida
Alpha Bank
LOS
Dodekanisos Ferry
Docking
To Petrol Station,
Petalo & Blue Star
Ferry Docking

War Memorial
NORTH QUAY

To Pitini &
Chorio

Manos
Petalo
Dolphin
SOUTH QUAY
Bridge
ANES Ferry Docking

Town Hall
Nautical
Museum
Town
Square
MID QUAY
Maria Boat
Hotel 1900
Pantelis
Yachta
Bus Stop
Taxi Boats
National Bank
Poseidon
Meet the Meat
Pachos
Taxis
Trata
Thea
Lazy Steps
Iapatos
Kokona
Old Markets
Mediterraneo
Bella Napoli
St John's Church
Kalistrata
Vapori & Harani Bars

Kataraktis
CHORIO
Village Square

The **Mid Quay** is where the taxi boats are moored along with the **Poseidon** and **Maria** 'round the island' boats. Along this wide quay there is the bronze statue of '**Michalakis** – the little fishing boy' by the local Symi artist Costas Valsamis as well as a sculpture of **Evgenia Mastoridou**, the first woman to dive (while pregnant) in a full diving suit in 1863 by Kalymnos sculptor Sakellaris Koutouzis. There is also a statue of **Stathis Hatzis**, the legendary 'naked diver', and two large black anchors, origin unknown.

Across the road, the quay is fronted by a mixture of shops and cafes as well as the **National Bank**. Here you can find the famous **Pachos Bar**, **Aigialos Café Bar**, **Eva's Cocktail Bar** and the **Perantzada** Bar as well as **Maria's Symi Boutique.**

Behind the mid quay are the lanes of Yialos which form the commercial heart of the harbour. As well as tavernas, there are many shops, supermarkets, the post office, bakeries, a laundry, newsagent, flower shop, boutiques, ice cream parlours and offices as well as some small hotels and the **Church of St John**.

The widest of the streets heading back from the harbour is at the southern end of the mid quay (opposite the black anchor). Here you will find the main shipping agent **Symi Tours** as well as a mixture of shops including **Akoumi** which specializes in traditional handmade food products of Symi and the **Sophia Gallery** which sells a good selection of jewellery, sculpture and art. There is also the famous **Leonidas Creperie** and at the end of the street **the Taverna O Meraklis**.

The Statue of Michalakis

Leaving the mid-quay, the road swerves inland towards the bridge where you will find the **Gefiraki Café**, the second **pharmacy**, the **Stavros** herb shop and the **Vasilis Taverna**. To the left as you cross the **Stone Bridge** (kaldirími) towards the north quay is the main **Town Square**, which has recently been developed into a marble amphitheatre and a car park (with limited spaces). Before the bridge was constructed, this square was a boatyard where many of Symi's famous skiffs are believed to have been constructed.

At the back of the square on the northern side is the **Town Hall**. Today the square is used regularly for events and festivals but in 1964 it was covered completely by a giant experimental 'solar still', a vast plastic covered concrete installation, funded by a 'friend of Symi' in the USA and developed by the Church World Service. Although the aim was sincere, there was nowhere to collect the fresh water and most residents had their own supply anyway, so the still was dismantled and the Symiots got their square back.

Once over the bridge, you reach the **North Quay,** or Mouraghio, with its sponge shops, bakery, tavernas, bars and boutiques. Straight ahead is the **Dolphin Pizzeria** (with **Symi Estate Agency** above), a **bakery and Panormitis Travel agency**. To the left are a number other bars and tavernas, the **Blue Lagoon** dive shop and the **Town Hall**.

To the right is **Dino's Sponge Shop**, **Mina's Boutique** and the **Manos Fish Taverna**. About halfway along you will find the **War Memorial/Monument**, carved into the rock and set back from the road, commemorating sacrifices made during the second world war. The inscription reads *"Today freedom spoke to me secretly. Cease, twelve islands, from being downcast. 8th May 1945"*. Every Sunday morning, soldiers based on Symi, raise the Greek flag at the memorial and then lower it in the evening.

A little further on from the War Monument, you pass **LOS** (Lobster, Oyster, Sushi) Bistro Bar and Art Gallery. This building, although recently expensively refurbished, was once a sponge factory and later the island's Town Hall. It was here in 1945 that General Wagner of the German occupying forces surrendered to the British. If you look between the two entrance doors to the building, there is a plaque, in English and Greek, which states, *"The surrender of the Dodecanese to the Allies was signed in this house on the 8th May 1945"*.

The Clock Tower

As you walk further on, past the **Alpha Bank**, **Elpida's Kafeneio,** the **Top Supermarket, Roloi Café** and **Glaros Car Rental** on the left and tied up yachts on the right, you eventually reach the famous **Clocktower** at the northern point of the harbour. Built in 1881, the Clocktower has survived more or less intact and is a great reference point. Dodekanisos ferries dock in this area and recently an immigration post has been set up to screen non-EU visitors arriving by boat. Opposite the Clocktower is the **Police Station**, which was built by the Italians for use as a Government building, during their occupation of the island.

As you round the point, passing the **Nireus Hotel** and various waterside restaurants, you enter **Harani Bay** and its boatyard, which is still in operation today. Carrying on past the boatyard you pass the **Carnagio Café** and then the ramp leading up to the **Evangelistria** church on the hill, then past **Odyssia** restaurant and apartments and you then reach the point of Harani Bay, **Tholos Restaurant**, and the **'Town Beach'** or 'Nos/Paradise Beach', as it is known. From here the road carries on to **Nimborio**, which is a 30-minute walk.

To reach Chorio, or 'the Village', requires quite a few steps or, alternatively, a quick hop on the bus or in a taxi. There are actually two main sets of steps up from Yialos, the famous Kali Strata and the lesser known Kataraktis, which rises from the back of the harbour.

The **Kali Strata** starts in Yialos with the blue steps behind the Bella Napoli restaurant (be sure to turn immediate left!) and rises up behind the Old Markets Hotel. It then widens out into a Grand Avenue. As you climb, you pass many of the grand mansions built when the island was at the peak of its prosperity. About two thirds of the way up you reach a 90-degree turn to the right, from where there are great views of the harbour from a helpfully placed bench. If you carry straight on here, you reach the road out of the village that leads to the **Windmills** and **Pontikokastro**.

If you turn right and carry on up the Kali Strata, passing the **Kali Strata** restaurant on the left, you eventually reach **George and Maria's** restaurant and two very welcome bars –the **Rainbow Bar** and **Lefteris Kafeneon.**

Above, and to the right of these two bars, is the village square, or **Syllogos Square**, which is used for festivals and other events. If you turn right and cross over the square following the road out on the other side, it will lead you past the **Lemonitsa Church** and around the Kastro, eventually connecting up with the **Kataraktis** steps, which lead back down into Yialos.

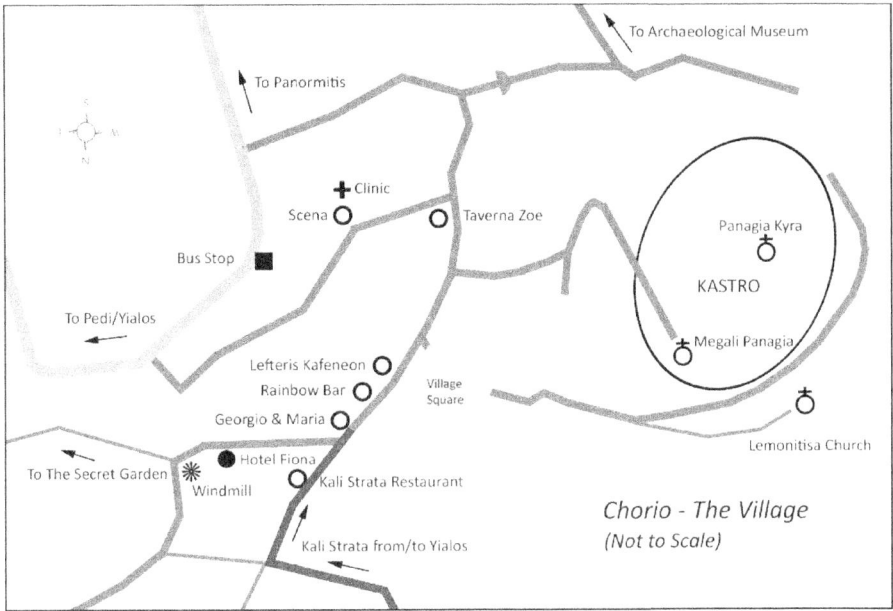

To Archaeological Museum

To Panormitis

Clinic

Scena

Taverna Zoe

Bus Stop

Panagia Kyra

KASTRO

To Pedi/Yialos

Lefteris Kafeneon

Rainbow Bar

Village Square

Megali Panagia

Georgio & Maria

To The Secret Garden

Hotel Fiona

Windmill

Kali Strata Restaurant

Lemonitisa Church

Kali Strata from/to Yialos

Chorio - The Village
(Not to Scale)

Alternatively carry on from the two bars straight through the village, passing the bakery and greengrocer and **Zoe's Taverna**. If you follow the somewhat haphazard signs, you will eventually reach the wonderful little **Archaeological Museum** (directions to the museum can be found in the 'Other Attractions' chapter).

If you turn right before Zoe's, this will lead you up to the **Kastro** and to the blue and white **Megali Panagia Church**, which has magnificent views over Yialos, Pedi and Turkey beyond. The path around the back of the church (through the courtyard) leads you round to the small stone chapel at the top of the hill (**Panagia Kyra**).

There are many churches in the village to explore and all have their own character. Some, including **Haritomeni Church** (on the way down from the Kastro) have wonderful examples of mosaic pebble courtyards or 'hokhlakia'.

Inevitably you will get lost in the village, but this adds to the charm. You can easily spend hours meandering through the labyrinth of lanes, admiring the many ruins, churches and views. On some of the ruins you can still see the original pigment used to colour the houses. If you are lost, just head downwards and you will eventually find the village or connect with either the Kali Strata or the **Kataraktis** steps back down to the harbour.

Haritomeni Church, Chorio

PEDI

The sleepy settlement of Pedi lines the lovely Pedi Bay, which is directly to the east of Symi's main harbour but separated by a headland (Noulia). It provides safe, sheltered anchorage, although it's nowhere near as popular as Yialos harbour with visiting yachts.

If you're looking for a peaceful area to stay but with the sea and beaches right on your doorstep, then this is the place to come.

It's also a lovely place to while away a languid afternoon with lunch and perhaps a few carafes of krasi in one of the excellent tavernas. Recently there has been a bit of a renaissance, with a new hotel and taverna opening up, but Pedi retains its charming soporific ambiance.

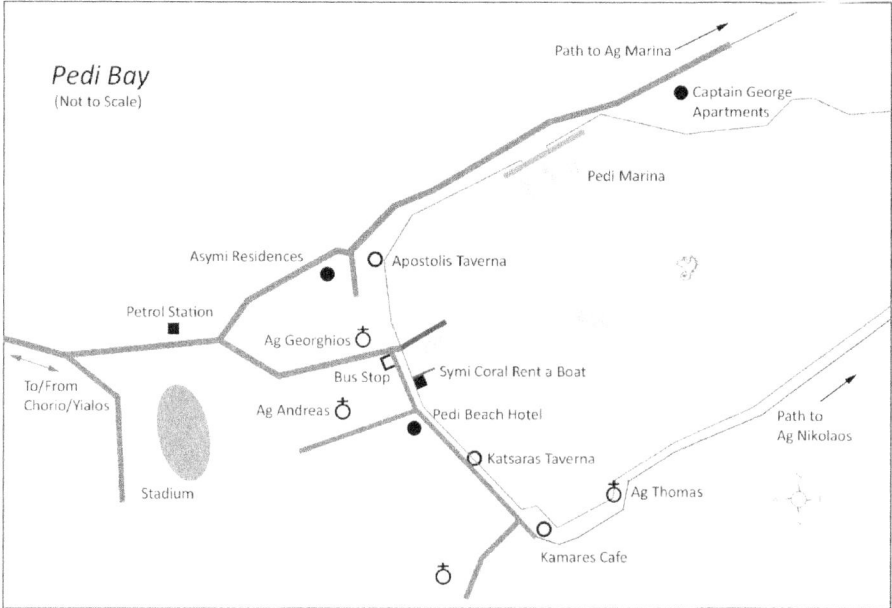

Pedi Bay
(Not to Scale)

Path to Ag Marina

Captain George
Apartments

Pedi Marina

Asymi Residences

Apostolis Taverna

Petrol Station

Ag Georghios

To/From
Chorio/Yialos

Bus Stop

Symi Coral Rent a Boat

Ag Andreas

Pedi Beach Hotel

Path to
Ag Nikolaos

Katsaras Taverna

Stadium

Ag Thomas

Kamares Cafe

A single road leads from Chorio for about a kilometre down the edge of the Pedi valley, past the power station to the bay where there is a jetty. A taxi boat service operates from here to Agia Marina and St Nicks beaches, both at the head of the bay. The Symi bus serves Pedi every hour in the summer with the main bus stop by the jetty (departures from Pedi on the half hour).

Turning left as you face the jetty takes you past the **Blue Corner Café** and a number of houses towards a small beach and the **Apostolis Taverna** ('Taverna Tolis'). In the winter this 'taverna' serves as a boat repair yard. Its conversion into a taverna seems to bear no relation to the 'season', but sometime, normally in June, tables appear and it officially achieves its metamorphosis.

Past Apostolis you meet the road that runs along the north side of the bay. To the left (behind Apostolis) is the newly developed **Asymi Residences** – a modern 4-star hotel and apartment complex.

Sleepy Pedi Bay

Carrying on along the north of the bay, you will come to the recently completed 'Symi Marina' (https://www.marina-symi.gr/), which has 50 berths for yachts with a draft of up to 8 metres as well as providing excellent facilities, including showers, water, electricity and even accommodation for rental.

Carrying on past the marina the road culminates in the colourful Captain George Apartments and the Irini Apartments. If you continue on the path between these two apartment complexes you will eventually reach the beach at Agia Marina but it's a hot, dusty trail with rocks and gravel, so be prepared.

Back at the jetty in the centre of the bay, but this time turning right, the road takes you past the dedicated jetty for 'Symi Coral Rent a Boat' (www.symicoral.gr) which offers powered boats to rent for the day so you can do your own exploring of Pedi Bay or further afield to one of the east coast beaches. No license is required, so after a 20-minute orientation/briefing you are on your way. Anna and Makis will pick you up from your hotel and deliver you to the jetty.

Further along you reach the Pedi Beach Hotel and a small supermarket. Opposite is the large and well-located (on the water) Katsaras Taverna, beach bar and beach (see 'where to Eat'), where the bus also stops having turned round on its way back to Chorio & Yialos. Carrying on just before the corner of the bay you will find the lovely Kamares Café, offering 'coffee, snacks and more', which has a nice location overlooking the bay.

Following the path around the corner to the left and along the south side of the bay you will pass a number of holiday apartments, boat moorings and the tiny chapel dedicated to **St Thomas**, and the path then continues all the way along the bay to St Nicks Beach (Agios Nikolaos) where you can catch a taxi boat back to Yialos.

Set back from the bay off the main road you will also find chapels dedicated to **St George** (at the road junction from Chorio), **St Andreas** (next to Pedi Beach Hotel) and the **Archangel Michael** (SW corner of the bay). Looking back from the bay the fertile Pedi valley rises up towards Chorio and beyond.

GETTING AROUND

Symi is a small island so if you are staying in Yialos or Chorio, walking (and climbing steps) is the best option. However, there is a bus as well as six (at the last count) taxis for those who need assistance, as well as car and bike hire agencies and of course the water taxis for access to the beaches.

There is a bus (singular) which travels on the hour (in summer months) from the bus stop on the south quay of the harbour in Yialos up to Chorio and then down to Pedi Bay, returning from there on the half hour. As well as the regular stops, the bus will also drop you anywhere on the route on request. The fare is €2.50 per person, payable on exit.

There are also a number of tour buses which go regularly to Panormitis, Marathounda and Toli Bay from Yialos and are bookable via **Symi Tours** on +30 22460 71307 (see http://www.symitours.com/ for further information). In addition to running the Symi bus, **Lakis Travel** (+30 22460 71695) also provides Symi bus excursions and offers car hire services, as does Panormitis Travel (+30 2246 070211).

There are 6 taxis on the island and the taxi rank is also on the southern quay of the harbour in Yialos (adjacent to Taverna Haris). Fares are reasonable (about €5.00) to go up to the village.

A recent innovation of the Mayor, the Symi 'Train' travels from its base by the main square in Yialos round the harbour to Nimborio (well not quite Nimborio actually, as that is a further 10 minutes on foot). It is incredibly 'touristy', plays Greek music (Zorba the Greek) loudly and is hated by many. However, children appear to love it, the driver is a hoot, and it provides an easy way of seeing some of the coast relatively quickly (a round trip takes about 40 minutes). The fare is around €8.00 per person.

Although a small island, it is certainly worth hiring some wheels for a day to look around, as there is plenty to see. There are a number of car/bike hire agencies, the largest being **Glaros Car & Bike Rentals**, located by the Clock Tower.

Fiat Panda cars can be rented for €30 (low season) to €50 (high season) per day & bikes €15-€30 per day. Further information at http://www.glarosrentacar.gr/ or contact +30 22460 71926.

Cars are also available to hire at **Lakis Travel** on the opposite side of the harbour, next to the taxi rank. Prices are similar to Glaros. Lakis Travel can be contacted on +30 22460 71695.

If you just require a scooter or motorbike, **Jimmy's Moto Rentals** on the south quay, close to the taxi rank, has a good selection from around €20 per day. Jimmy's can be contacted on (+30) 22460 72110.

There are two petrol stations - one on the extreme east side of the harbour on the southern quay (turn left just before the road leaves Yialos) and the other on the road down to Pedi Bay. Around €15 of petrol should be sufficient for a day trip round the island in a Panda.

For information on water taxi services/beach boats, see the following section on beaches.

TWO EASY WALKS

Symi is noted for its large variety of excellent walking trails and is very popular with hikers during the cooler shoulder season months of May and September/October. This is serious stuff though and not the subject of this book!

However, for those that would like a 'not too difficult', 'not too long' relaxing walk as part of their holiday, there are lots of options, two of which are outlined here.

The first walk takes you from central Yialos to the beach settlement of Nimborio. There are two routes. One route goes inland and 'over the hill', whilst the second route runs along the coast. Each leg is about 30-40 minutes (the hill route is a little shorter) and makes a good round circuit with a nice lunch and some sunbathing in the middle.

Start by heading out of the main square in Yialos towards the west (away from the harbour), past **Iapetos Village Hotel** on your left. Follow the road out of the town, bearing slightly right up the steep incline until you reach a church on the left at the top with a churchyard (**Agios Elikoni**) enclosed by a long white wall.

Keeping the wall to your left, take the left turn at the fork onto the path (if you go right on the road you end up at the helipad!) and follow the path past the various smallholdings and goats over the hill and eventually on to a further church (**Agios Georghios**) on the left. This church which is normally open (you need to work out the latch on the gate) provides stunning views over Nimborio Bay from its lovely arched wall.

Agios Georghios Church

From here you can glimpse the enticing colour of the water down in Nimborio. Just follow the path as it zig-zags down to the main road. When you reach the main road turn left onto it opposite the yellow door and you will soon pass **Giala,** which is a popular beach with a kiosk serving ice cream and snacks. Keep going on the main road and follow this for a further 10-minutes or so until you reach the **Metapontis** beach taverna and the **Amalthea Snack Bar** at **Nimborio**.

After lunch you can either return the same way or perhaps more likely, just continue on the relatively flat coastal road all the way back to the clock tower and Yialos where a cool drink awaits. Alternatively, you can take the taxi-boat back.

The second walk starts at the bottom of the **Kali Strata** which is located behind the Bella Napoli pizza restaurant in Yialos. It takes about 30 minutes, depending on how fast you can climb! Take the blue steps behind the restaurant and immediately turn left, following them up the Kali Strata past the **Old Markets Hotel** as it opens out into a grand stepped 'boulevard'.

After stopping to catch your breath at the bench with a view near the top, carry on to the right up the steps to the **Kali Strata Restaurant** and then turn left before the **George & Maria restaurant.**

Follow the road down past the supermarket on your right and the **Fiona Hotel** on your left until you reach the **Windmill**. Turn right here and follow the path all the way down the hill to the main road.

Turn left on the main road, past the **Secret Garden** and the road junction and continue straight on all the way down the road, passing the **Power Station** on your right, and the desalination plant and petrol station on your left until you reach the settlement at **Pedi Bay**. When the road emerges at the jetty on the seafront you have a choice of turning left or right. Luckily there are good tavernas in both directions!

If you turn right, past the Pedi Beach Hotel and **Katsaras** Taverna (see 'Where to Eat'), you can follow the path further all the way round the bay, past the **Kamares Café** to the beach at **St Nicholas** where you can catch a taxi boat back to Yialos. If you turn left, you can enjoy a good lunch at the **Apostolis Taverna** and then you can catch the bus back to Yialos or Chorio from the jetty.

Katsaras Restaurant, Pedi

SYMI BEACHES

I f you are coming to Symi for the beaches, then don't expect vast golden stretches of sand like those in Thailand or Australia. Symi doesn't do big beaches.

What Symi does excel at are a number of small, intimate, quaint coves, some with sandy beaches and some with pebble beaches and each one unique and beautiful in its own way. Nearly all of the beaches also have excellent tavernas.

Getting to these beaches is part of the fun and one of the most exhilarating aspects of visiting Symi. Beach boats or 'water taxis' from Yialos serve most of them, and some can also be reached by beach boat from Pedi. Some can also be reached by road or by footpath.

The main beach boat operator is **Taxi Boats Symi** operated by Konstantinos, Michael, Loukas and Irini since 1978 with their distinctive orange and white livery. These boats serve the beaches on the east coast of the Island, typically departing Yialos at 10:00, 11:00 and 12:00 and returning at 15:00, 16:00 and 17:00 (return times vary by beach so check on departure). Fares range from around €11.00 return to Agia Marina to €16.00 return to Marathounda.

Another operator, **Symi Taxi Boats**, operated by Pavlos & Kostas, also serves the main beaches from Yialos at similar departure times to the boats of Loukas & Irini. These boats also serve Nimborio beach, which is not currently served by Taxi Boats Symi.

Should you wish to visit more than one beach, or some that are inaccessible by water taxi, the excellent and very popular **'Poseidon Round the Island'** tour is the thing for you. The Poseidon departs daily (from the harbour adjacent to the water taxis) at around 10:30 and takes a slightly different route each day around the island returning at about 17:00. It costs around €50 per person which includes an excellent buffet lunch. Great value and a great day out. Further information at http://www.symi-excursions.gr/

In 2018 a similar day excursion was launched using a traditional Symi fishing caique. The excellent **Maria Traditional Boat** visits many hard-to-reach bays on Symi and visits a different part of the island each day. Day trips include a buffet lunch for around €45 per person. The boat can be booked on the mid quay or via Lakis Travel or tel +30 22460 71695. Further information at facebook page @mariaboatsymi.

Another excursion boat, the lovely caique **'Victor Minas'** **(https://victorminas.gr/)** owned and operated by Giorgos Tsavaris also regularly takes parties around the island. Book via the website or call +30 694 289 8500.

Finally, the **Aegean Star** also does similar trips around the island and can be booked as a private charter via +30 694 647 8546.

If you prefer to see beaches from the 'bottom up', so to speak, then why not try scuba diving with **Blue Lagoon Divers** who have a variety of dive sites around the island and offer PADI training courses. They have a dive shop next to the Town Hall in Yialos so drop in or contact Will Zoyroydis on+30 694 758 3862.

A **top tip** before setting out for Symi's beaches is to purchase a pair of rubber soled swim shoes. These are invaluable at the pebbly beaches, enabling you to coolly slip into the water and also to sprint out of the sea quickly to rescue your belongings from marauding goats!

The main east coast beaches (in order of travel by boat from Yialos) and their main characteristics are described below.

AGIA MARINA (SANDY)

This is the first stop from Yialos and only a 10-minute taxi boat ride. It is a beautiful location with aquamarine waters and a sandy-bottomed bay. The sandy beach overlooks a tiny island on which is located the picturesque Agia Marina chapel, a popular setting for weddings, which you can swim across to in only a few minutes (although make sure you look out for approaching boats when swimming across).

The area behind the beach has a large sunbathing platform with lots of sun beds and umbrellas (chargeable) and behind that is a lovely taverna with a separate bar and seating area, fronted by a gorgeous deep purple bougainvillea.

Marina is probably the 'chicest' of the beaches on Symi, having been developed initially by a French/Italian couple in a very stylish way.

The taverna, although being one of the most expensive, provides high quality food in a lovely setting looking out across the bay.

Agia Marina has recently changed ownership and is now part of the group that also owns the Iapatos Hotel in Yialos and the Niriides Hotel in Nimborio. Significant investment has been made in the facilities including new sunbeds, infrastructure, free wifi and beautiful planting and the beach now has very much a 'beachclub' vibe. The facility can also be hired for weddings.

Agia Marina

The improvements have brought an inevitable increase in sunbed prices which vary from €25 per person for 'VIP' beds to €15pp for 'front row beds', €10 for 'normal' beds or €5-8pp for unshaded beds (2023 prices). Sunbed pricing has become quite the trend recently throughout Greece, although there has been significant pushback from local groups in some areas.

As well as boats from Yialos, this beach is also served by beach boats from Pedi and you can also walk from Pedi, following the path along the north side of Pedi Bay, or from Chorio, following the path that follows the ridge by the deserted windmills and Pontikokastro.

AGIOS NIKOLAOS 'ST NICKS' (SAND & SHINGLE)

The second stop on the taxi boat route from Yialos, Agios Nikolaos, better known as St Nicholas or 'St Nicks' is a sandy/gravelly cove located on the south side of Pedi Bay adjacent to the chapel of Aghios Nikolaos.

Again, this beach is a mix of sand and shingle and has lots of lovely tamarisk trees which provide natural shade. There is a large shallow area for swimming and sun beds and umbrellas can be hired. This beach tends to be very popular, given its close proximity to Yialos and Pedi, its shade and sandy beach.

The Beach at Agios Nikolaos

The taverna here is very good, and staff extremely helpful. It offers a selection of Greek specialities and there is a separate small bar/coffee area for drinks in the centre of the beach. Sunbeds here are around €5 per person per bed (2023 price).

This beach is also accessible by foot, by following the footpath along the southern shore of Pedi Bay. The beach boat from Pedi also calls here at regular intervals.

NANOU (PEBBLES)

Nanou is a lovely long stretch of pebbles (bring your rubber shoes) backed by high cliffs and fronted by crystal clear water. There is a substantial shallow area for swimming and snorkeling and, due to its length, it never seems that busy, although it is a popular spot, especially amongst serious sun worshippers, some of whom sometimes swim 'alfresco' at the far end of the beach.

Nanou Bay

There is an excellent taverna located in the centre of the beach, serving Greek dishes. It is also popular with the local goats, who roam the beach and will bug you for the odd morsel through the taverna fence.

Some welcome new umbrellas and sun beds have recently appeared and are available for rent (at a discount if you eat in the Taverna). In 2023 sunbeds were around €3 per person and the taverna was also open in the evenings and accessible by boat.

It is possible to walk to Nanou, although it is not as straightforward as walking to Marina or St Nicks as you need to drive to where the (steep) path down to the beach leaves the main Yialos to Panormitis road just before the War Memorial.

AGIOS GEORGIOS OR 'ST GEORGE' (PEBBLES)

St George's beach is probably the most dramatic beach on Symi as it is backed by a 300-metre cliff face. As there are no facilities, it is a beach for 'purists', and only accessible by boat. Because of this it tends to be served less frequently by the taxi boat operators. The colour of the water here is something special and the swimming is really excellent.

The small chapel of St George is the only building and apart from that the beach is an unspoiled sweep of pebbles. Due to the high cliff this beach tends to lose the sun before the others. Be sure to take your own food and water!

During the busy summer months, it is possible to 'beach hop' with Taxi Boats Symi. You can spend a few hours at St George and then go on to another beach for lunch!

MARATHOUNDA (LARGE PEBBLES)

A personal favourite, Marathounda Bay is the last stop on the taxi boat schedule, with only one service per day (outbound from Yialos at 11.00, returning at approximately 16:45).

Marathounda is simple and rustic but a lovely bay with large pebbles (rubber shoes are definitely required here) and probably the clearest (and coldest) sea water bathing around the island - very invigorating, but don't let that put you off. The water is relatively cold due to the presence of an underwater cold spring on the north side of the bay. If you swim on the north side, be prepared to encounter some icy water!

Sun beds and umbrellas are provided (€3 per person at the taverna but free if you arrive via Taxi Boats Symi) and there are a few large tamarisk trees which provide welcome shade, although you'll have to be quick to nab a spot here.

There is an excellent taverna, which can get quite busy, serving Greek food including their special goat in lemon sauce. Those goats lucky enough to survive the pot roam the beach, eating tourists' belongings and generally making a nuisance of themselves. This is highly entertaining, especially at lunch time when they surround the taverna begging for scraps.

A small coffee bar **'Kyma'** has recently re-opened adjacent to the taverna, offering drinks, light meals, burgers etc.

There are also a number of villas and rooms adjacent to the taverna which are available to rent through **Angel Holidays** and other agencies.

Marathounda is also accessible by road and many visitors stop here following a visit to the Monastery at Panormitis, which is just 5 minutes away by car. If you are driving here be warned (from personal experience!) not to park under the trees as the goats will climb all over (and damage) your car to get to the branches above!

Marathounda Bay

NOS (GRAVEL)

Nos or 'Paradise Beach' is the 'town' beach, being closest to, and walkable from, Yialos in about 15 minutes from the town centre (just follow the road around the north side of the harbour).

It is the remarkable creation of one man and his wheelbarrow, the late indomitable Dimitris, who could be seen rearranging the gravel at the end of each day to preserve the beach. He also constructed a beautiful garden at the back of the beach with cacti and a range of other plants as well as a waterfall and ran a very successful taverna on the water's edge.

Due to its proximity to town, Nos has always been very popular, catering for residents, day trippers from Rhodes and even local shop and restaurant workers who grab a quick swim and some sun in-between shifts.

Unfortunately, since Dimitris is no longer with us the beach has fallen into disrepair and the facilities have closed (although the beach itself is still accessible). It is hoped that a new operator will be found for this popular beach for the 2024 season.

NIMBORIO (GRAVEL)

Many people love Nimborio because it is quiet and occupies a lovely location in a large bay to the west of Yialos. It is accessible either by taxi boat (Symi Taxi Boats at approx €5.00 each way) or by road. The Symi 'train' also goes most of the way from Yialos to Nimborio, although it is a good 10-minute walk from where it drops you to the beach. To walk from the clock tower takes approximately 30 minutes and you can also walk via the 'back road' out of Yialos (this walk is explained in the 'Getting Around' chapter).

The settlement of Nimborio is quite spread out and you pass a couple of other beaches (including the excellent and very welcome refreshment kiosk at **Giala**) before reaching the final one which has a number of tamarisk trees for shade and the old-fashioned family-run **Metapontis** taverna offering a warm welcome and a traditional Greek menu. Sun beds and umbrellas are available (chargeable) on a recently refurbished gravel beach.

Next door can be found the recently opened **Amalthea Snack Bar** which serves a range of drinks and snacks and has luxurious sunbeds and deckchairs available for rent (free with a minimum spend of €15pp in 2023). Amalthea also has luxurious apartments available above for rent.

From the beach you can walk around the bay, visiting a couple of churches culminating in **Agios Merkourios chapel** on the north side which offers a good view back across to Nimborio (although the structure was unfortunately badly damaged by a landslide in late 2019).

There is also an interesting church (early Christian Basilica) at Nimborio with a **mosaic** in its courtyard which may be from a Roman villa or building which previously occupied this site. To find this continue along the beach (past the wall) until you reach a dry river bed on the left (with black water pipes on the surface). Turn left here and passing a small church on your right you will see a path and some steps up to another church on your left. Proceed up to this church by the main gate and the mosaic can be seen to the right (north) of the church, covered by a corrugated roof. It will most likely be partially obscured by leaves & debris, which you can brush aside & a splash of water will enhance the colours and reveal the pictures.

Further to the back of this same church are a number of dank, vaulted catacombs which can be accessed by what is basically a hole in the ground. These may have been burial chambers.

PEDI (PEBBLES & SHINGLE)

Many people love Pedi Bay as it tends to be quieter than Yialos in the Summer.

There are two main shingle beaches at Pedi, one towards the north side of the bay by the simple but very good, taverna **Apostolis**, which has free sun beds, and one adjacent to the **Katsaras** taverna, which is towards the south side of the bay. The Katsaras taverna is also excellent, if a little expensive, and occupies a lovely position jutting out into the bay. It usually has a good selection of seafood. The owners have recently added an adjacent beach bar. Sun beds and umbrellas are available for hire. Across the road there is a small supermarket.

The popular **Pedi Beach Hotel** is close to both the bus stop and the boat quay in the centre of the bay.

Pedi Bay is walkable from Chorio in about 30 minutes (see the chapter on 'Getting Around') and the bus serves the bay hourly on the half hour during the summer.

TOLI BAY (PEBBLES)

Toli Bay lies on the western side of the island and the prevailing onshore winds and swell make it difficult to operate a reliable water taxi service, although some boats do go there when possible.

It's a beautiful spot surrounded by Oleander trees ('Dafnes') with a long thin pebbly beach and views across to St Emilianos. Sun beds and umbrellas are available at no charge. The beach is not the best on Symi but there is something about the lovely location that makes it idyllic. Swimming here is good and the water normally warmer than on the eastern side of the island.

Taverna **Dafnes**, located above the beach is one of the best on Symi, offering Greek food as well as some more sophisticated dishes. The food is excellent. Make sure you buy some of their delicious honey to take home!

Thankfully Toli is accessible by road - there is a signed turn to the right off the main Yialos-Panormitis road as you approach the top of the hill out of Yialos. Just keep following the 'Toli' signs and keep going until you descend steeply into Toli Bay.

Recently a bus service has also started (contact Symi Tours at +61 2246071307) if you don't want to drive there. This will drop you there in the morning and then pick you up in the afternoon, giving sufficient time for some swimming, a nice lunch and a snooze! Now that the road has been paved all the way, the taxis will also take you, although they are significantly more expensive than the bus.

Toli Bay

OTHER ATTRACTIONS

THE KALI STRATA

The **Kali Strata** or 'Good Street' is the grand stepped 'boulevard' linking the harbour and Yialos with the village of Chorio. It is well worth making the climb at least once during your visit.

Kali Strata

It starts with the blue steps behind the Bella Napoli restaurant on the south side of the harbour, passes up behind the Old Markets hotel and then widens out, passing some of the grand neo-classical mansions that were built in the 19th Century when Symi enjoyed its period of maximum prosperity. It is thought that the Kali Strata itself dates from around 1850. Many of the mansions probably belonged to Captains of the sponge diving boats or rich merchants of the time. Sadly, some of them are now ruins, although many have been refurbished. One of the larger mansions is the three storey 'Russian House', set back to the right of the Kali Strata (about halfway up) which was built in 1914 and which commands panoramic views of the harbour.

There are about 400 steps up to the village square at the top and a nice viewpoint of the harbour towards the upper section where the street does a 90-degree turn. About halfway up, Maria often awaits to offer you 'free' refreshment in return for selling you some dried herbs that you didn't know you needed. Close to the top you pass the Kali Strata Restaurant and then two very welcome bars.

THE ACROPOLIS/KASTRO

The **Kastro**, as it is known today, towers over both the harbour and Chorio itself. Its origins are multifarious, but it is thought that some form of acropolis or citadel has been on the site since Neolithic and Pelasgic (pre-Greek) times as some of the walls (believed to be of Pelasgian origin) are still visible. The site has been built on for centuries by various visiting tribes - Classical, Roman, Byzantine, Italian/Venetian and Turkish but it was the Knights Hospitaller who, having a knack for fortifications, built up much of what can be seen today during their time on the island (1309-1522). Indeed, the crest of arms of Pierre d'Aubusson (the Knights' Grand Master) remains in-situ high up on the southern wall (there is also a similar crest in the archaeological museum).

There are also three churches within the immediate confines of the Kastro - two small chapels and the larger blue and white church of **Megali Panagia**. Up until 1944 there was another church - the Church of the Assumption of the Virgin Mary (Panagia), just to the south and slightly below the existing Church. Adjacent to this Church were merchants houses and storerooms and it was here that German troops stashed munitions and detonated them at the end of the war, completely destroying the church and its surroundings.

The Megali Panagia Church

Since then the existing Church has taken the title of Megali (greater) Panagia. From here there are fantastic views of the harbour and down to Pedi. Mounted on the wall to the left of the main door there are two crests from the period of the Knights.

In common with many churches on Symi, the Church has a flag pole resembling a ship's mast, a reminder of the island's links with the sea.

Outside the church, to the left of the entrance, are two bells, one of which is formed from the nose cone of a 1,000-kilo bomb. Inside the church there is a 16th Century artwork by the Cretan artist Giorgios Klontzas entitled 'the Icon of the Second Coming'.

If you follow the path around the church you can walk all the way round and up to the small stone chapel, **Panagia Kyra**, on the very top of the Kastro, which is believed to have been built on an ancient Temple to Athena. Although it is locked, the views of the harbour are particularly good from here.

Panagia Kyra

PONTIKOKASTRO & THE WINDMILLS

Looking up from the harbour towards the village, a number of derelict windmills are clearly visible along the ridge of the hill. Less clear, unless specifically looked for, is the large round stone circle to the left of the last windmill, known as **Pontikokastro** (the Mouse castle).

It is worth a trip up to Pontikokastro for one of the best views of the harbours of both Yialos and Pedi (easily done by bus or on foot). The structure itself is made of a number of massive stones, all cut with precision and laid in a large circle with a domed roof. The origins of Pontikokastro are unknown, but some say it could be a monument to King Nireus, or even that he could be buried there. Other rumours suggest that there could be a tunnel from Pontikokastro to the main Kastro in order to forewarn of approaching enemies!

Pontikokastro

As for the windmills, or **Myloi**, they were used to mill grains of wheat and barley until imported flour put them out of use. Some of those nearer the village have been refurbished into dwellings and one (nearest the Kali Strata) was, until recently, a very good restaurant called, unsurprisingly, 'the Windmill'.

Where the main road up from the harbour crests the hill by the windmills there is an interesting monument to **Pierrot**, the white pantomime figure that has appeared in European theatre for many years. Legend has it that the Pierrot character was fashioned on a local Symiot who had been observed by Venetian visitors 'larking around' outside the windmills as long ago as 1500. A Danish pantomime producer who visited the island in 1992 researched the story and the plaque (in Greek and English) now commemorates Symi's gift of Pierrot to the world!

PANORMITIS

Visitors to the island may struggle to understand the reverence in which this Monastery (officially called the **Monastery of the Taxiarchis Michael Panormitis**), and its Archangel, St Michael, Patron Saint of Symi, is held amongst Symiots, as well as amongst other Dodecanese islanders and southern Greeks. A total of nine monasteries on Symi are devoted to St Michael, of which Panormitis is the largest.

St Michael is seen as the 'Protector' of Symi and is particularly relevant to sea-faring folk. Indeed, many of the sponge diving boats used to call at Panormitis to be blessed before heading off on their long summer journeys.

The site is so important that every year, in November, thousands of pilgrims and vendors descend upon the Monastery for the Panormitis Festival. Even the ferries abandon Yialos and sail directly from Rhodes to Panormitis for these very special few days ('Panormitis Day' is the 8th of November) and many hotels on the island remain open until then before closing up for the winter. The Monastery site is transformed with a plethora of stalls and traders selling their wares. It's quite the jamboree! Somewhat bizarrely, many pilgrims can be seen carrying brooms as an offering to St Michael as legend has it that monks heard him sweeping the Monastery at night.

The Monastery at Panormitis

The Monastery, which sits on a beautiful turquoise elliptical bay, at the southern end of the island (at the end of the road from Yialos), is built on an ancient temple of

Poseidon, the original 'God' of the sea and seafarers. Much of the building seen today was constructed in the 1780s and consists of a chapel (1783), two museums, a library, a gift shop, a grocery, a bakery, and administrative offices. Additional buildings to each side, providing basic accommodation for pilgrims, were added later. The most striking feature is the beautiful large central bell tower which was built in 1905.

The central courtyard is covered by a beautiful mosaic of black and white pebbles (hokhlakia) and contains the small chapel of St Michael. Allow your eyes to adjust to the dark interior and you will be able to make out the vaulted ceiling, rich artwork, wooden carvings and the marble pillars which are believed to be all that remains of the original Temple of Poseidon. The paintings are by two local monks, Neophytos and Kyriakos Karakosti. The revered silver-plated icon of St Michael (created in 1794) can be found here on the right-hand wall just before the small exit at the rear.

Either side of the chapel there are two museums - one displays religious art and a collection of items (including messages in bottles and model boats) washed into the harbour, whilst the other is a folklore museum with furnishings and fabrics from early Symi life as well as a number of amphora, probably used in wine production on the island. There is a small entry fee of a few euros.

The visitor may wonder why they have paid to enter a museum full of rather tatty model boats and other 'stuff' washed ashore, but these items have all been washed into the bay at Panormitis 'by God's hand'. Within the sea around the Dodecanese islands are a number of currents which cause items to drift into this particular bay. Thus, countless generations have written 'messages' to St Michael and attached these to model boats or other items or sealed them in bottles and set them afloat around Symi. If they arrive at Panormitis, it is a sign that St Michael will grant their wishes and the items are collected and displayed in the museum.

There are two other tales worth recounting regarding the Monastery here - one sad and one uplifting and both associated with the Second World War.

During the war, the Monastery was used as a listening post for allied communications and in 1944 German troops discovered British commandoes and a radio transmitter at Panormitis. The British were taken prisoner but their Symiot 'assistants', the Abbot and two others, were found guilty of collusion and were executed by firing squad. This terrible event is commemorated at Panormitis by a memorial to Abbot Chrysanthos Maroudakis, Mihailis Lambrou and Floros Zochangellis who 'Laid down their lives for the cause of liberty' on 11th February

1944. The memorial is in the Monastery grounds near the entrance and there is also a room devoted to them in the museum.

The second tale involves a young monk who, in 1943, was travelling on a troop ship from Patmos to Symi when it was torpedoed and sank. Clinging to driftwood, he prayed to St Michael, and vowed that if he survived, he would devote the rest of his life to the Church. Luckily, he was rescued and returned to Patmos. However, after the tragic execution of the Abbot at Panormitis, and the looting of the Monastery by German troops, he was sent to Symi.

He then worked single-handedly to revive the Monastery, which was by then in a very poor condition. His tireless work has resulted in the Monastery we see today and the facilities and administration capable of supporting the thousands of pilgrims who visit every year.

To visit Panormitis, you can hire a car or bike, take a taxi or take the bus which travels regularly from Yialos (see the section on 'Getting Around'). Some ferries from Rhodes also call at Panormitis before travelling on to Yialos, enabling sufficient time for a visit.

If you have time, as well as visiting the Monastery, take the walk to the windmill at the mouth of Panormitis Bay (on the right when facing out to sea). It's a lovely walk round the bay which is beautifully landscaped, and which provides lovely views back across to the Monastery itself.

THE CASTLE MONASTERY OF ST MICHAEL ROUKOUNIOTES

The impressive Monastery of **St Michael Roukouniotes** is also dedicated to the island's Patron Saint, is often overlooked by visitors but it is rich in history and artwork. It is the second largest, after Panormitis.

Architecturally, it is the oldest and most important monastic complex on Symi. It is believed that the earliest structures were built in the 5th Century on a pagan site but most of what can be seen today, dates originally from the 15th Century at the time of the Knights. It features a 'double' chapel in its centre (a newer 18th Century chapel built over an older 15th Century one), surrounded by other monastic rooms and walls which were fortified in the 18th and 19th Centuries.

The lower, older, chapel has a pebble floor and 15th Century wall paintings, but the upper chapel is richer in terms of religious art. It has an intricate pebble and stone mosaic floor, complex wood carving, and contains the early 17th Century icons of Archangel Michael and of the Hospitality of Abraham, believed to be by Emmanuel Yendes, as well as wonderful frescoes by the local artist Gregory of Symi, painted in 1738.

In the 18th Century, the Monastery used to accommodate around 80 monks and contains a refectory, an oven, storerooms and quarters for the Abbot and monks. Outside there is an olive grove, olive press, stables, a cistern and a flour mill.

The complex has recently been beautifully refurbished with the help of funding from the European Union. The upper chapel is still used sometimes but the complex has no official opening times.

To reach the site, take the main Yialos to Panormitis road and at the top of the climb out of Yialos take the road to the right signed to Toli Bay until you reach an ancient Cypress tree on the left surrounded by a low, circular, white wall. The Monastery is adjacent to the tree, which is believed to be centuries old.

Both Symi Tours and Lakis Travel feature the Monastery on their day excursion trips to Panormitis (contact details can be found in the 'Practicalities' section of the book).

THE MONASTERY OF ST MICHAEL KOKKIMIDES

The small Monastery of **St Michael Kokkimides** is well worth a visit if you have time. It is much smaller than those at either Panormitis or Roukouniotes but it has an exquisite and richly decorated small chapel.

You can reach Kokkimides either on foot or by car as there is a good, but steep, road and a large car park. You will need to open the large vehicle gates (and close them after you). From here there are fantastic views across to Turkey on a clear day. Enter the complex via the door adjacent to the car park (under the bell) and immediately to your left you will see a small brown metal door. This is the entrance to the tiny chapel.

Inside there is a black and white pebble floor and some lovely wall paintings, thought to be by local Symi artists.

Although it is thought that the original Monastery on this site dates from the 9th Century AD, the building was extensively renovated in 1697. Behind the Monastery is a large, and ancient Cypress tree.

To reach the Monastery by road, take the Yialos to Panormitis road. After climbing out of the village, past the radio station and heading south, you will pass a turning to the left to the communications tower. Immediately after this there is a further turning on the left with a small sign to Kokkimides. Follow this road for some distance to the next junction, turning right. Passing a number of other churches, the road winds its way up and you will finally reach the Monastery.

A Painting from the Chapel of St Michael Kokkimides

BYZANTINE WINE PRESSES

As well as shipbuilding and sponge-diving, Symi was also well-known for producing a delectable white wine during the Byzantine period (and probably for many years before then). The evidence for this can be found in the discovery of over 130 stone **wine-presses**, distributed throughout the interior of the island, which can still be seen today. They have been thoroughly researched and some have even been rebuilt by local resident historian Sarantis Kritikos, who has published his findings in a book 'The Stone Wine Presses of Symi', available on the island.

The best examples of the presses can be found in the Kourkouniotis area. To reach this, take the main road from Yialos to Panormitis. After passing the War Memorial on the left you will reach the small monastery of **Meghalos Sotiris**, on the right.

Park here and follow the path/road on the opposite side of the main road from the monastery (you will see a yellow non-directional sign saying 'Byzantine stone wine presses'). As you go down the path, you need to turn almost immediately right past a small, fenced enclosure and follow the path that leads through the pine forest.

You will pass a number of piles of stones which 'could be' wine presses but keep going and this lovely shady walk will eventually bring you to a reconstructed wine press below a severely battered and almost illegible sign. If you carry on a little further, you will reach the monastery of Michael Korkouniotis nestling in the woods. Allow about 15 mins each way.

THE DRAKOS ANCIENT EDIFICE

The Drakos or Drakou ancient edifice ('dragon's lair) is an ancient edifice located towards the lower southern slopes of the Pedi valley. Its origins are unknown but parts of it are believed to date back to the 4th century BC. It consists of a walled enclosure (now capped) with individual structures within, although the site is overgrown and filled with accumulated earth. There are a number of clean-cut blocks and columns but it's difficult to navigate the site. It's thought that the building is from the neolithic period and was probably related to the agriculture of the time. It's certainly no Pompeii but something to tick off your Symi list!

There are two ways to reach the site. As you take the main road up through Chorio towards Panormitis, beyond the sports centre (but before the first hairpin bend), you will see a sign to the left and this path eventually leads to the site.

Personally, I prefer to access the site from the Pedi Road. From this road (as you go down towards Pedi) you will see a turning on the right just before the power station. This road leads you to the stadium which you need to walk around (on the

Pedi side). Keep following the road as it passes the stadium and keep going straight on past a boatyard on the left and up the hill past a church on the right. Follow this road/path as it bends up the hill. Eventually it runs out at a house but just before the right turn into the house you will see a path with a gate that leads straight up along a dry river valley.

Go through this gate and up the valley until you reach a junction. You will see blue dot markers, and this is where the Chorio path enters from the right. Turn left here and follow the narrow path past a wall with blue paint in places and through two rickety gates (please close them behind you!). Shortly beyond the second gate you will find the monument (there is a sign which is no longer standing). Watch out for some pretty vicious thistles along the path as well as snakes, spiders and goats around the monument! The distance from the main Pedi Road is about 1.5km.

THE MONASTERY OF ZOODOCHOS PIGHI

The Monastery of Zoodhochos Pighi is set high up above the southern slopes of the Pedi valley (directly above the Drakos Edifice). It has stunning views over Pedi and the valley and also back to Chorio and, on a clear day, beyond to Datca in Turkey. It's definitely worth a visit for the views and is accessible either on foot or by car.

The most striking feature is the magnificent walled vegetable garden just below the main building which contains orange trees and a number of seasonal crops. There is also a separate walled garden beside the Monastery where fig trees are cultivated.

These gardens are possible because there is a natural spring which emanates from a cave behind the Monastery, and this is used to irrigate the crops. The name of the Monastery literally means 'life giving spring'.

At the far end of the courtyard there is a recessed area and a tap where you can sample the cool clean water from the spring. This is particularly welcome after the trek to the Monastery on a hot summer day!

The water is then piped down to Chorio via the black plastic pipes you can see by the main gate but is considerably warmer by the time it reaches the village!

The walled garden at Zoodochos Pighi

To reach the Monastery take the main road through Chorio towards Panormitis. After the second hairpin bend you will pass a kantina on the left and shortly thereafter a sign pointing left to Agia Marina church. Take this turning and the road will take you past Agia Marina and its cemetery and on up to the Monastery. It's about 1.5km from the main road.

If you are walking, it's a hot trek so be prepared. There isn't much in the way of shade until you reach a large and welcome tree just before the final ascent. The spring water at the Monastery seems particularly tempting at this point!

If you're feeling adventurous, there is a very rough path (hardly discernable) which leads beyond the Monastery and on to the abandoned agricultural settlement of **Gria**.

ST EMILIANOS

In a bay on the north-west coast of the island is the **Monastery of Agios Emilianos**, which lies in a beautiful setting on an islet at the end of a short promontory. Before the Monastery was built, it is thought that the crews of the sponge diving fleets gathered on this site before setting out on their journeys.

The Monastery was built in the mid-19th Century by a family who grew rich on the fortunes of the sponge diving trade. It was the tradition then for richer families to construct and donate such buildings to the Church which then sanctified them.

From the sea the Monastery looks quite large, but the interior is small containing an unadorned chapel and some rooms which can be rented. It has been refurbished relatively recently following a lightning strike! Its main attribute is its beautiful setting. It is also a poignant place as the islet bears the inconspicuous tomb of a young girl from Kalymnos, who is believed to have met her death here in 1942.

The Monastery can be reached by footpath for avid walkers but the easiest way to reach it is to take the daily 'round the island' cruise on the Poseidon (or the Maria), which often makes a stop here for lunch before heading to the Fokospilia grotto for swimming. Be sure to check on which days the Poseidon and Maria stop there.

Agios Emilianos Monastery

CHURCH OF AGHIOS IOANNIS PRÓDROMOS (ST JOHN)

With over 180 churches, chapels and monasteries on the island you are never far from God! You can't miss the **Church of St John** as you wander through the lanes of Yialos.

The church, which is the second largest on Symi dates from 1868 and has a fine black and white mosaic pebble courtyard surrounded by mature trees entwined with bougainvillea. At the northern entrance to the site there is a substantial bell tower (illuminated at night) and, in common with many churches on Symi, a ship's mast, signifying the island's links with the sea.

During the war a bomb fell through the roof of the church, although it didn't explode, and just outside the gate to the south, there is a second world war gun embedded in a rock.

St John's courtyard, which contains a wonderful example of hokhlakia pebble mosaic, is also one of the venues used for the annual **Symi Festival**, which runs during the summer months and features a number of musical and dance performances throughout the island.

ARCHAEOLOGICAL MUSEUM

It is well worth making the trek up the Kali Strata and all the way through the village to visit this wonderful little museum which documents the history, life and art of Symi. Once in the village, follow the central street (the continuation of the Kali Strata) and follow the signs for quite some distance (approx 5 min walk from the village square).

As well as explaining the shipbuilding and sponge-diving industries, it contains a number of interesting artefacts, including a stone carved coat of arms of the Knights Hospitaller Grand Master Pierre d'Aubusson (1476-1490) from the Kastro and also a selection of historic coins from the same period, all found on the Island. It also documents the religious painting of the Island.

Open Monday to Sunday 08:30 to 15:30 (closed Tuesdays). At the time of writing, entrance €4.00.

Many people get lost when looking for the archaeological museum, which can be frustrating, so here is a step-by-step guide: -

1. From the top of the Kali Strata keep walking straight through the village, past the two bars on your left and straight on until you reach Taverna Zoe, also on the left (museum sign on the wall on the right).

2. Keep going straight on, past the greengrocer on the right until you reach a junction with a path to the right.

3. Turn right here (museum sign on wall ahead) and pass immediately under a lovely stone arch and then immediately turn to the left by the telegraph pole (sign is on the left, which you can't see coming from Chorio, so this is where most people go wrong!).

4. Carry on past a yellow house & bougainvillea on the left & zig zag past another bulbous yellow house on the right.

5. Keep going straight on until you reach a T-junction with a ruined arched door ahead of you (museum sign above window) - turn right here!

6. Carry on past a house with a yellow wall until faced by two ruins. Turn left here (sign is on right as you turn).

7. Now zigzag along a bit until you reach another T-junction fronted by a 3-storey white house with blue shutters. Turn right and then immediately left (sign on wall).

8. Follow the steps upwards and you will finally reach a small square with the museum on your left.

CULTURAL EVENTS

For a small island, Symi has a number of regular cultural events to keep you entertained.

During the summer months there are regular musical performances up in the village at **George & Maria's Taverna**, the **Secret Garden, Scena Restaurant** and at **Constantinos View**. Down in the harbour, **Elpida's Kafeneion** often has live music and many impromptu 'bouzouki sessions' pop up every now and then in many of the tavernas.

The annual **Symi Festival** takes place between July and September and features a comprehensive programme of music, dance, theatre, film and food at various venues throughout the island.

The **Symi International Film Festival** (http://www.symifilmgroup.com/) is part of the Symi Festival and screens a programme of films, normally in September.

There is also a regular film club with screenings at the **Lefteris Kafeneon** up in the village.

Keep an eye on local postings for further information on these events.

WHERE TO STAY

There is a wide variety of accommodation on Symi to suit every budget and taste. This ranges from hotels to apartments and villas to rent to simple rooms to let. Whatever the type of accommodation you choose, even the most basic rooms on Symi are generally very clean and well presented.

Most of the hotels and apartments are listed on booking sites such as booking.com and Expedia. There are also an ever-increasing number of properties on Symi available via Airbnb. Prices vary according to season and are generally cheaper before June and after September. Whilst there is a good quantity of accommodation available, it does fill up in the peak months of June–September when reservations are essential.

Houses, villas and rooms are also available to rent via the excellent **Angel Holidays** (previously Kalodoukas Holidays) at https://www.angelholidays.gr/en/ which can also assist with hotel stopovers in Rhodes, ferry tickets and transfers. Try also, **Select Symi** (https://www.selectsymi.com/) which features a small selection of hotels and apartments. Unfortunately, Symi Visitor Accommodation, which was the other main accommodation agency on Symi stopped trading in 2018.

If you are travelling with a tour operator such as Olympic Holidays, they also have a good selection of hotels and apartments to suit everyone.

Please remember that water is in limited supply on Symi and although tourist establishments have priority, please conserve it wherever possible.

Some of the more popular establishments are listed below: -

THE OLD MARKETS

A luxurious and sympathetic conversion of the Old Market building or Agora in Yialos, this exclusive boutique hotel is probably the finest on the island. The five rooms have been beautifully crafted and retain many period features and the suite is outstanding. Although not all rooms feature sea views, there is a lovely, elevated terrace with views over the harbour. A separate building to the rear of the property offers an additional 5 rooms in the Captain's Mansion which are each themed around sea voyages and maritime history. Prices range from €200 to €495 per night. As well as the Old Markets, Andrew and his team also run the **Emporio** Hotel in Nimborio (see later listing). Further information at https://theoldmarkets.com/.

THEA

Five beautiful modern air-conditioned apartments have been created in this restored 1913 neoclassical Symi mansion by the lovely and very welcoming Chatzistratis family. Rooms are modern and top notch, and all have wonderful views over the harbour. Located adjacent to The Old Markets. There are no 'hotel' facilities as such, but breakfast supplies are provided. The two larger rooms on the upper floor are split level and can accommodate up to 4 people. Plans are afoot to increase the number of rooms with the development of the property next door. Prices range from €100 to €220 per night. Further information at http://www.symi-thea.gr/

HOTEL 1900

Hotel 1900 is a new addition to Symi's growing number of quality hotels. It is located on the south quay in a neoclassical listed building known as the 'Mastoridis Mansion' (after the famous sponge diver – see earlier section on Boatbuilding and Sponge Diving). It has been sympathetically refurbished by architect Dimitris Zografos and retains many period features, including magnificent ceilings once found in many Symi mansions. Four beautifully decorated and appointed suites vary in price between €150 and €425 per night depending on room chosen and season. Minimum stay 3 nights. Further information at https://1900hotel.com/ +306944623284.

Hotel 1900 can also be booked via https://selectsymi.com/ which also features the **Limani Life** apartments adjacent to the clock tower (€50 to €250 per night) and the beautiful and secluded 'On the Rocks' apartment in Nimborio, which is perfect for a romantic escape.

NIREUS HOTEL

The Nireus Hotel, next to the clock tower in Yialos is something of an institution. Its 36 air-conditioned rooms are simply furnished but clean. Some have (small) balconies and those at the front of the hotel are highly coveted with people booking a year ahead. The view out to sea and of the harbour entrance from these rooms is exceptional - count yourself lucky if you bag one. 'Town view' rooms at the back are disappointing in comparison, particularly those on the ground floor (but cheaper).

The Nireus also has a good restaurant serving Greek favourites with tables right on the water and a small jetty which is the perfect location for a sun downer. Steps from here lead into the sea and are a popular place for a quick dip when temperatures soar.

Prices approximately €130 to €150 per night for a sea view room (less for rooms at the rear). Rooms are also available via tour operators such as Olympic Holidays. Further information at http://www.nireus-hotel.gr/ Didn't open for the 2020 season.

IAPATOS VILLAGE HOTEL

Iapatos Village is a modern hotel set in beautifully landscaped gardens towards the back of the harbour area in Yialos. Rooms are contained in 25 neoclassical houses. Some rooms are split level, and some have balconies or verandas as well as kitchenettes. The hotel has no sea views but makes up for this by having one of the few swimming pools on the island as well as a sauna. Rooms are arranged around a courtyard and there is an excellent bar and restaurant. Rates vary from €105 per night in the low season up to €275 per night for a suite in the high season. Some of the maisonettes can also accommodate up to six people at additional cost. Iapatos has the same owners as **Niirides** Hotel in Nimborio (see below). Further information at http://www.iapetos-village.gr/

ODYSSIA APARTMENTS

This lovely establishment run by the friendly Morari family is located in Harani (a 10-minute walk from the clock tower) with lovely views across Harani Bay to the Yialos and Chorio. Apartment rooms are simply furnished but good value. Some are split level and have kitchenettes. All have access to a large terrace with lovely views. The onsite restaurant is also excellent. Prices are €50 to €105 per night. Further information at http://www.symi-odyssia.gr/index.php

ANASTASIA

The family-run Anastasia hotel in Yialos is a real gem if you want simple, spotlessly clean and very affordable accommodation in a fantastic location. Nestled behind the clock tower and the Nireus Hotel, Anastasia can be found 40 steps above the quay, directly opposite where the ferry docks. Each of the air-conditioned rooms has a private bathroom with shower and some rooms have recently been modernised with beautiful new bathrooms. Rooms at the top have views but are accessible via a spiral staircase so pack lightly! There is also a courtyard and some rooms have balconies/use of a shared terrace. Prices from €60 per night. Further information at http://www.anastasiahotel-simi.gr/

KOKONA

The recently and tastefully refurbished **Kokona** is a small hotel adjacent to St John's church and the clinic in the middle of the town of Yialos. It has 10 rooms with modernised en-suite bathrooms, some with a balcony. Breakfast is served in a shady courtyard next to the bell tower of the church. Proximity to the church means that the bells can be intrusive on occasion. Take your earplugs! Prices approximately €70 to €110 per night. Further information at http://www.symigreece.com/kokona.htm

HOTEL FIONA (CHORIO)

This modest, quaint, blue and white-themed hotel commands lovely views from its location close to the top of the Kali Strata. Run by Fiona and Michaelis, it has 14 recently refurbished air-conditioned rooms, all with en-suite facilities and many with balconies enjoying sea views. It also has three adjacent studios next to the hotel for rental. The hotel can also be reached by road from Yialos if you don't feel up to tackling the steps. Breakfast is included in the rates. Prices from approximately €55 per night. Further information at http://hotelfiona.com/

EMPORIO (NIMBORIO)

Emporio has been developed by the same team behind the Old Markets Hotel. Situated in quiet Nimborio, about three kilometres from Yialos, this villa offers luxury solitude and is perfect for birthdays, weddings and special occasions or just as a luxury family escape. It features four incredibly stylish bedrooms, one 2-bedroom unit and a lovely cottage with amazing sea and garden views, all set in wonderfully landscaped gardens. From 2023, Emporio will only be available to rent for exclusive use i.e., the whole villa.

Prices are likely to start at around €700 per night. Further information at https://www.emporiosymi.com/ or +30 695 730 2565.

NIRIIDES (NIMBORIO)

Also located in the lovely quiet neighbourhood of Nimborio, the Niriides Hotel and Apartments is arranged over five buildings overlooking Nimborio Bay. All have recently renovated modern bathrooms. Rates vary from €140 per night for a standard room to €240 per night for a villa in the high season, inclusive of breakfast. There is a bar and evening meals are provided from a lovely (but limited) menu in a wonderful garden overlooking the beach at Giala. Non-residents are welcome. Bear in mind there are limited dining options available in Nimborio itself, although the hotel offers a shuttle service to and from Yialos on request. This hotel is now part of the same group that also owns the Iapatos Hotel in Yialos and the beach taverna at

Agia Marina. Further information at http://www.niriideshotel.com/ or +30 2246 071784.

PEDI BEACH HOTEL (PEDI)

This hotel appeals to those perhaps looking for a quieter retreat. Located at the head of the lovely Pedi Bay (3km from Yialos) it has 56 all en-suite rooms with either a sea or mountain view. Rooms are nicely furnished in blue and white. There is a sun terrace with sun beds but no pool although the sea (and a small beach) is just across the road from the hotel. The hotel provides a shuttle service to Yialos. Prices vary from €54 to €159 per night depending on season and view. The hotel can also be booked via some tour operators. Further information at http://www.pedibeachhotel.gr/index.php

'On the Rocks' Apartment, Nimborio (see 1900 Hotel)

WHERE TO EAT & DRINK

Visitors are certainly not spoilt for choice when it comes to eating establishments on Symi. There is a wide selection of restaurants and tavernas around the harbour, although the choice is more limited up in the village.

There are also a number of bars/coffee shops dotted around so you are never far from a refreshing Mythos or Alpha beer, a carafe of Greek wine, an ouzo, a Greek coffee or whatever takes your fancy.

For those self-catering or perhaps on a lower budget there are a number of 'take away' food outlets, including two excellent bakeries and supermarkets.

Although restaurants come and go, some popular restaurants and bars at the time of writing are listed below, although everyone eventually finds their favourite establishments.

Wherever you go, be sure to try a plate of the famous and delicious **Symi Shrimps**, which are eaten whole, including the shell.

Here are some other Greek dishes to try: -

Baklava	Honey and nut filo pastry desert
Dolmades	Vine leaves stiffed with rice & herbs (& sometimes meat)
Gemista	Tomato & pepper stuffed with rice (& sometimes meat)
Gigantes	Large broad beans cooked in a tomato-based stew
Gyro	Grilled meat normally served in a pitta bread
Fava	Fava beans – pureed and served hot or cold with onion
Imam	Fried aubergine topped with tomato/onions/garlic & feta
Kleftiko	Slow-cooked lamb in foil with garlic/tomato/herbs/potato
Mezedes	A selection of small plates of food

Saganaki	Small-pan dishes often cooked with Greek cheese
Soutzoukakia	Meatballs in tomato sauce
Souvlaki	Pork/chicken/fish grilled on a skewer
Spanakopita	Spinach pie often made with filo pastry
Stifado	Beef stew with garlic/small onion/tomato & herbs
Tuna Salad	Beware this is usually NOT a salad! Tuna-mayo
Zucchini Balls	Fried courgette/Zucchini patties

Tzatziki	3.00	Pork suvlaki	10.00
Tuna fish salad	3.00	Chicken suvlaki	10.00
Eggplant salad	3.00	Pork chops	10.00
Saganaki cheese	5.00	Veal chops	12.00
Cheese pie	5.00	Pork fillet	10.00
Spinach pie	5.00	Beef burgers	8.00
Stuffed vine leaves	8.00	Fillet steak	16.00
Cheese balls	5.00	Pepper steak	18.00
Baby marrow balls	5.00	Bacon	8.00
Steamed mussels	8.00	Sausage	8.00
Halumi cheese	5.00	Beef stifado	9.00
Bekri meze	10.00	Lamb chops	10.00
Cod fish	8.00	Lamb kleftiko	10.00
Salmon	6.00	Lamb with pasta	9.00
Oktopus salad	10.00	Moussaka	8.00
Small shrimps	13.00	Stuffed tomatoes	8.00
Saganaki shrimps	18.00	Stewed meat balls	8.00
Shrimps N°1	18.00	Pastitsio	8.00
Kalamaris	13.00	Mix meat for 2 persons	20.00
Sword fish suvlaki	13.00	Green beans	4.00
Sole fish	13.00	Broad beans	4.00
Fish fillet	13.00	Briam	4.00
Red mullets	50.00	Imam	5.00
Red snapper	50.00	Greek salad	5.00
Sea bream kil.	50.00	Beet root salad	5.00
Lobster kil	65.00	Boiled greens	5.00
Mix fish for 2 persons	50.00	Cheese salad	5.00

A Typical Symi Menu

PANTELIS

On the southern quay, Pantelis is ever popular with lots of tables outside directly adjacent to the harbour where yachts and gulets tie up. A buzzy atmosphere ensues in the height of the season. Specialises in seafood (seafood risotto and seafood pasta are excellent) but offers a range of dishes with large portions and friendly service.

Pork dishes are particularly good with the meat from Pantelis's own farm on the island. Try the pork stew with wine & onions! Pricing: Moderate. Tel: +30 2246 07211.

HARITOMENI

Set halfway up the hill behind the south quay, this restaurant commands incredible views of the harbour and beyond from its lovely outdoor terrace. A good choice of fresh fish, grilled dishes and mezes feature but it is the view that is the main attraction here. Pricing: Moderate. Tel +30 2246 072771.

MEET THE MEAT

Previously the ever popular To Spitiko restaurant on the southern quay, now transformed into a traditional grill house, the lovely Jordana still pulls punters into this recently expanded and ever popular family run taverna. As the name suggests, the menu is predominantly meat-based with souvlaki, gyros, burgers and grilled meat dishes but also with a selection of vegetarian dishes and salads and grilled cheeses. Pricing: Inexpensive. Tel: +30 2246 072452. Facebook @MeetTheMeatSymi

NERAIDA

This excellent restaurant can get overlooked by visitors as it is tucked away at the back of the lanes in Yialos but it is worth seeking out for reliable Greek food and reasonable prices. It also has a large covered 'outdoor' area at the back, decorated with local murals and is popular with locals. All the regular dishes are featured – Kleftiko, Moussaka, fish, Kalamari as well as mezes, salads, souvlaki etc. Try the cheese balls – excellent! Pricing: Moderate. Tel: +30 2246 071841.

PETALO

On the southern quay, all the way along next to the petrol station, this beach bar and restaurant is a welcome addition to the Symi scene. Located on the water's edge, with sunbeds and lounge chairs, this is a nice place to while away the day at an 'alternative beach' with a good vibe. Choose from a beach or restaurant menu, both featuring excellent wines. Good salads and a variety of Greek and other dishes with a twist! Try the Athenian Salad! Pricing: Moderate. Tel: +30 2246 072389 or facebook @petalofoodbar At the time of writing, it is unknown whether Petalo will open in 2024 as the decking used for the 'beach' was deemed to be illegally constructed and has been removed. We await to see whether any facilities will be available on the site.

YACHTA

A new addition to the scene in 2019, 'Yachta' occupies the site of the former Mythos restaurant on the south quay. Owned by Pantelis it has been refurbished to a very high standard and retains a fantastic ambience – a lovely place to be! The food is essentially 'up market' Greek and mainly seafood based (including a selection of ceviche/carpaccio), although some meat and vegetarian dishes feature. Pricing: On the expensive side. Tel: +30 2246 0721.

TRATA TRAWLER

'The Trawler' is a Symi institution. Located at the southern end of Yialos and set back from the harbour in the lanes, it offers a wide range of traditional Greek dishes such as lamb kleftiko, beef stifado, souvlaki, saganaki as well as fresh fish and seafood. Family run and Inexpensive. Tel: +30 2246 071411.

BELLA NAPOLI

Located in the lanes at the foot of the famous Kali Strata, this 'Italian' trattoria/pizzeria offers large wood-fired pizzas, pasta and salad dishes. A change from the ubiquitous Greek fare offered at most other restaurants. Tables are set outside adjacent to the Vapori bar, so music is a constant companion. Take away available. Pricing: Moderate. Tel: +30 2246 072508 or +30 2246 072456.

SEAME

A new addition to the scene in 2023, Seame is a lovely small al-fresco restaurant and bar located in the lanes of Yialos where Vapori Bar used to be located. The lovely Marina serves traditional Greek fare as well as seafood and meat delicacies from a small adjacent kitchen. Tel: +30 694 754 6224.

DOLPHIN PIZZA

Located just over the bridge on the north side of the harbour, Dolphin serves pizza, pasta and salads from this small but friendly family pizzeria. Pasta sauces here are really excellent. Take away available. Pricing: Inexpensive. Tel: +30 2246 071149. https://dolphin-pizzeria.business.site/

MANOS FISH TAVERNA

Located under the famous green awning on the north quay, Manos fish restaurant is particularly popular with visiting Turks and celebrities and is known perhaps more for entertainment than food. Things can get loud with dancing and plate smashing in high season. Pricing: Expensive (and you have to pay for the plates). Tel: +30 2246 072429.

ODYSSIA

Located in Harani (a 10-minute walk from the clock tower), family run Odyssia (which also offers accommodation) is worth the walk. Friendly service and top-quality food presented with flair at reasonable prices. Offering a good choice of seafood and other dishes. The feta in filo is particularly good and Amberjack fillet is a speciality. Lovely views across the bay to Yialos. Pricing: Moderate. Tel: +30 2246 071210. http://www.symi-odyssia.gr/

THOLOS

Just past Odyssia and on the point of Harani Bay, Tholos occupies an enviably romantic location with tables by the sea affording lovely views back across to Yialos and the Kastro. Haroula and her team conjure up excellent dishes from a small kitchen across the road. High quality Greek meat, fish and vegetable dishes are on the menu as well as pasta and salads. The lemon potatoes are particularly good as are the fava beans and the gigantes. Vegetarians will find plenty to suit. Reservations recommended in high season. Pricing: Moderate. Tel: +30 2246 072033.

TAVERNA GEORGIO & MARIA (CHORIO)

A few steps further up from the Olive Tree, 'George and Maria' occupies a large mosaic floored courtyard on the left at the top of the Kali Strata. Known for its atmospheric live Greek bouzouki music and dancing on Friday and Saturday evenings (from 9pm) perhaps more for the quality of food or service. Very traditional Greek food with meat or fish dishes and 'mezedes'. Menu varies according to availability. Reservations recommended on Fridays and Saturdays in high season. Pricing: Inexpensive to Moderate. Tel: +30 2246 071984.

ZOE TAVERNA (CHORIO)

Taverna Zoe is in the heart of Chorio village and has a lovely terrace overlooking Pedi Bay. Simple, traditional Symi home cooking with a view, offering fish, meat and vegetable dishes. Pricing: Inexpensive. Tel: +30 2246 072520.

SCENA (CHORIO)

A welcome addition to Chorio's dining scene, Scena Café Bar Restaurant is popular with locals. Perched high up (just around the corner from Zoe's) with views over the village and down the Pedi valley it covers all bases offering a wide range of food including some international dishes, pizza, pasta, salads, mezedes, cakes, coffee, cocktails and drinks. There is often live music on Saturdays. Pricing: Inexpensive. Tel +30 2246 070020.

CONSTANTINOS VIEW (CHORIO)

If you want the best view of Symi (and beyond) from a restaurant/kantina, then this is the place to go! It's located some distance out from Chorio, high up on the main road to Panormitis so a bit of a trek on foot but easily accessible by car or taxi. It seems to have been constructed from whatever was available at the time, but this enhances the quirkiness. The specialty is grilled meat, souvlaki and burgers and it is very popular with locals. There is often live music on Saturdays. Pricing: Inexpensive. Tel +30 694 942 2776.

RESTAURANT BAR KATSARAS (PEDI)

Set in an enviable location built out into Pedi Bay, Katsaras is a large taverna offering quality food and a small beach bar adjacent to a beach area where sunbeds can be hired. Open for lunch and dinner, its location over the water makes it a lovely venue at any time of day, although evenings are a favourite. Worth a trip on the bus or a taxi if you're not staying in Pedi. An added bonus is that a bus stop right next to the taverna. Apart from fish and a number of Greek dishes, the special salad is particularly good, as is the cheesy garlic pitta bread yum yum. Pricing: Moderate. Tel +30 2246 071417. Facebook @katsarasrestaurant

TAVERNA TOLIS (PEDI)

Located to the north side of Pedi Bay (turn left as the road enters Pedi) this simple but lovely taverna serves up Greek favourites in what, during the winter months, becomes a boatyard. The timing of its metamorphosis into a taverna varies year by year but it is generally open during the peak summer months. Popular with locals and visitors, it offers good quality dishes at reasonable prices. A favourite! Tel +30 2246 071601. https://taverna-tolis.business.site/

BARS/KAFENEONS

There is no shortage of establishments in Yialos or Chorio for quenching your thirst and everyone eventually finds their favourite place.

Some of the most welcome places are those at the top of the Kali Strata. After all, who doesn't need a nice cold beer after slogging up 400 steps in the midday heat? Close to the top you pass the **Kali Strata Restaurant** on your left and then a few steps further up are **Lefteris Kafeneon** and the **Rainbow Bar**, which are both good shady places to cool off.

Down in Yialos you are spoilt for choice from the many bars and cafes fronting the harbour. **Mediterraneo,** adjacent to where the taxi boats dock, is a good place to sit and watch the daily hubbub unfold. **L'Alegrito** next door offers good value. Opposite the taxi boats stand is the **Aigialos Café Bar** (with its comfy chairs) and the legendary **Pachos** bar, favoured by locals and tourists alike for its reasonably priced drinks. Further along towards the bridge is **Eva's Cocktail Bar**, which is well known for its cocktails as well as **Perantzada Bar**.

Just around the corner from Mediterraneo is the main main 'late night' bar – **Harani Bar**, which plays extremely loud music into the small hours and is probably as close to 'revelling' as you can get on Symi! The adjacent Vapori Bar sadly closed in 2022 after many years of music competition with Harani Bar!

On the north quay, close to the clock tower, **Elpida's Café** is a popular spot with locals and visitors for a drink, cakes and meze, whilst watching the ferries and boats come and go. On Friday nights there is often live music and Elpida's bar snacks are particularly good!

A little further round, past the clocktower and on the path to Harani is the lovely (but expensive) **Tsati Bar**. With its pastel-coloured tables and chairs, it has a beautiful location right on the water's edge with views across to Harani and is open until late. Around the corner, just past the boatyard is **Carnagio Café**, which also has a lovely view from its outdoor tables.

Back up in the village on the road to Pedi, the **Secret Garden** is worth seeking out for drinks and mezes in a lovely courtyard. Run by Katya and Michaelis, there is also live music every Friday night.

The View from Tsati Bar

SHOPPING & THINGS TO BUY

For a small island, Symi has an excellent variety and number of shops, especially in the Summer season. Most of these are in Yialos, either along the harbour road or in the lanes towards the back of the town.

Good things to buy to take home include sponges, hammam beach towels, 'evil eye' charms, local honey, Symi sea salt, dried herbs and other local souvenirs.

SPONGES

Symi is of course famous for its sponges and although these are no longer harvested around the island, there are a number of shops selling them. Sponges make excellent gifts as they are light and easy to carry. They come in a number of 'grades' from soft to very abrasive, depending on your preference. There are three main sponge shops. The **Panormitis Sponge Shop** by the Town Hall is well known for its good selection of natural sponges. **Dinos Sponge Shop**, just over the bridge on the north quay also offers a fine selection, as does **Mikes Sponges** slightly further along. To the side of Dinos, there is an alleyway with some pictures of sponge-diving in its heyday and associated paraphernalia arranged around a small caique full of sponges.

SYMI PRODUCE

In the lanes of Yialos, **Akoumi** sells a range of local traditional handmade products including honey, marmalades, pastries, biscuits, wine, oil, herbs, pickles, figs and many other delicacies.

A good selection of herbs and spices can be found at the **Stavros** herb shop which is located just to the south side of the bridge in Yialos. Although not all from Symi, they make excellent gifts and are light to carry.

Symi Sea Salt has recently made its debut onto the culinary scene of the island. Created by an entrepreneurial couple and made in the traditional way by evaporation of sea water, it's now available in a variety of 'flavours' (mixed with various herbs, chilli and spices) and has become extremely popular. It is widely sold on the island.

LEATHER

In past years when the population of Symi was much larger, there used to be a number of leather merchants on the island, and even a tannery. Now only one leather shop remains on the north quay of the harbour. **Takis Leather Fashion** produces beautiful bags, shoes, sandals, clothing and accessories. The charming Takis Psarros is also an excellent artist producing beautiful intricate artwork using a fascinating technique of burning dots onto the leather to create vistas of Symi and other scenes. Be sure to visit his gallery next to the shop and he will be happy to show you around. http://www.takisleatherfashion.com/

ART & PHOTOGRAPHY

There are a number of small shops selling art and crafts but most produce is imported. For genuine art seek out Natasha at **Natali Art Studio** who, although originally from Russia, has lived on Symi for many years. Natasha paints scenes of Symi, often on driftwood, olivewood or antique pieces and has also produced many of the hand painted signs and murals you will see on buildings around the island. She has a small gallery and shop, selling her art and crafts as well as some interesting antiques, on the north quay of the harbour, next to Takis.

Resident artist **Marcia Whitworth** also paints local scenes and useful objects including doorstops and bottle holders that make excellent souvenirs. You can track her down via her 'Marcia Whitworth Paintings' facebook page or via Instagram @marciawhitworth

The **Sophia Gallery** in the lanes of Yialos also has a selection of sculptures as well as artworks and jewellery.

Symi is of course remarkably photogenic and you will take home with you many gorgeous photographs of your own. However, should you want to buy professional prints resident photographer and graphic designer Jord Blakesley produces some stunning imagery available via his website at http://www.symiart.com

CLOTHING & JEWELLERY

Clothing boutiques are ubiquitous in Yialos stocking everything from simple summer chic to high end labels and designer wear. Prices vary significantly so wander around and see what grabs you.

High end fashion pieces can be found at **Mina's Boutique** just north of the bridge. In the lanes are **Pandora** (Pandora jewellery and fashion) and **Americana** (which carries a number of brands) and further along is **Artemis**, which specializes in lovely Italian Antica Sartoria pieces.

On the mid-quay, opposite the taxi boats, check out **Maria's Symi Boutique** for competitively priced fashion, hats and bags as well as the excellent **Iliaxtida** boutique on the corner next to Mediterraneo.

Back from the front, around the start of the Kali Strata are **Symi Silver** (next to Bella Napoli Restaurant), which specialises in jewellery as well as fashion items, and up the steps adjacent to the Trata Trawler is **Xrisallis** Boutique, which has fashion inspired by the shop's French owner.

There are also a number of jewellery shops selling both fashion jewellery and individually designed pieces, some of which are made on Symi.

On the north quay, there is a small jewellery shop called **Chrisochoos**, a business founded by Dimitri Chrisochoo in 1850. The building itself dates from 1890 and became a workshop in 1900 (note the sign outside). It has been owned by the same family ever since. It is worth popping into this lovely building to look at the handmade and Greek-designer jewellery but also to admire the portraits of the family ancestors which adorn the walls.

It's also worth checking out the **Loukidis jewellery shop** next to the Trata Trawler restaurant in central Yialos. This has some lovely pieces, which you can often watch being created on the spot!

PRACTICALITIES

BANKS & ATMS

There are two banks in Yialos. Both have 24-hour ATMs. The **National Bank** is located opposite the taxi boats on the mid quay and the **Alpha Bank** is located along the north quay, past the war monument. Opening hours are generally 08:00-14:30 Monday to Friday. There are also other ATMs in Yialos, including one on the south quay near the pharmacy. The currency of Greece is the Euro.

BOAT HIRE

Powered boats can be hired at 'Symi Coral Rent a Boat', based in Pedi Bay. No license is required, and a full briefing is given prior to hire. Pick up from hotels is available and prices depend on length of hire (www.symicoral.gr). Tel +30 69575 48298.

Symibluewater RentaBoat also offers day boat rental from the clocktower. Contact via Lakis Travel on +30 22460 71695.

Boats are also available for hire from 'Rent Boat Yiannis' (https://rentaboatsymi.gr) located adjacent to the clock tower. Tel +30 6936880176.

CREDIT CARDS

Credit cards have to be accepted by law, although cash is often preferred. Problems sometimes occur with credit card authorisation links so carrying some cash is always recommended.

DOCTOR

The main clinic is now located in Chorio, underneath Scena restaurant and adjacent to the village bus stop (there is no longer a clinic in Yialos). The emergency number is +30 2246 071290.

It is well staffed but bear in mind that any serious conditions need to be treated at the hospital in Rhodes at the mercy of ferries, although helicopter evacuation is sometimes used in emergency situations.

ELECTRICITY

Electricity is 220 volts and the plugs are European 2-pin. Be aware that power cuts do occur occasionally.

HEALTH WARNINGS

The summer sun is extremely fierce in Symi and the temperatures are high. Be sure to take precautions, including the use of sunscreen and hats, and keep hydrated. Other irritants include mosquitoes (although Symi mosquitoes don't seem to be as troublesome as those in Rhodes) and sea urchins, which are common around the rocky coast. The use of rubber shoes when swimming is recommended, and these can be purchased on the island.

LANGUAGE

You will find that many Greeks speak English and some working in the tourist industry will also speak at least some commonly used phrases in a number of other languages as well.

However, it always helps to know a few simple words in Greek and Greeks always appreciate it and will be happy to help you with further words and pronunciation. Here are a few words to get you started!

Good Morning	Kaliméra
Good Afternoon	Kalispéra
Good Night	Kaliníkta
Yes	Ne
No	Óhi
Thank you (very much)	Efharistó (polý)
Please/You're welcome	Parakaló
Hello (to one/many)	Yassou/Yassas
How are you?	Tí Kánis?
Good	Kalá
Sorry	Sygnómi
How much?	Pósso?
The bill (please)	Ton logariasmó (parakaló)
Cheers!	Yamas!

MOBILE PHONE COVERAGE

Although the Greek cellular service (both Cosmote and WIND) is widely available, the location of the island means that Turkish mobile services can also be picked up in places. If you do not wish to pick these up then disable 'automatic roaming' and select COSMOTE.GR or WIND.GR manually.

PHARMACY

There are two pharmacies, both in Yialos. One is just to the south of the bridge (Tel +30 22460 72050) and the other is on the south quay just before the taxi station (Tel +30 22460 71888). Opening hours are 09:00–13:00 and 17:00 21:30 Monday to Saturday but during the summer season the pharmacy near the taxi rank is open all day from 08:30–22:00.

POST OFFICE

The Post Office is located at the back of the lanes in Yialos.

POLICE

The Police station is next to the clocktower. There is little known crime on the island. Tel +30 22460 71111.

SCUBA DIVING

A recent and very welcome addition to Symi's recreational scene is **Blue Lagoon Divers**. Owned and operated by Will Zoyroydis the company provides a range of PADI courses and recreational dives for qualified divers in a variety of locations around the island. The dive shop is located at the back of the main square in Yialos near the Town Hall. Further information at https://bluelagoondives.com/ Tel +30 694 758 3862.

SHIPPING AGENCIES

There are a number of agencies which can arrange tours and bookings. **Symi Tours** (Tel +30 22460 71307/771689), located in the lanes of Yialos just back from the mid quay, can make (and change) ferry bookings for Blue Star, Dodekanisos and ANES.

Other agencies for ferries, trips around the island, car rental etc include **Lakis Travel** (+30 22460 71695), located on the south quay next to the taxi stand (Lakis also operates the Symi bus and the Maria Traditional boat) and also **Panormitis Travel** (Tel +30 22460 70211), located just north of the bridge.

SUPERMARKETS

For those staying in self-catering accommodation, or on boats, there are a number of supermarkets, in the lanes of Yialos, including **Georgina's Market** (Tel +30 22460 71660) and **Taxas Supermarket** (+30 22460 71375). Both deliver supplies to boats. Recently a swish '**Top Market**' supermarket has appeared on the north quay near the clock tower, which has become known as the 'Waitrose of Symi'.

VETERINARY SERVICES

There is a pet shop (Pet Island Symi) located at the bottom of the Kali Strata. A vet visits from a Rhodes clinic regularly. Tel +30 693 447 2839.

You will notice that Symi, like many Greek islands has more cats than it knows what to do with and the majority are feral. A recent initiative 'The Symi Neutering Programme' (SNiP) has been set up with charity funding and the help of Symi Animal Welfare (https://symianimalwelfare.org/) to deal with this problem. Tel +30 693 725 2279.

WATER

The water from the taps is not potable but bottled water is widely available on the island. Please remember that water is extremely scarce and has to be de-salinated or shipped in from Rhodes, so use it sparingly. Ice can be bought, somewhat bizarrely, at the bakery on the north side of the bridge.

WI-FI

Free Wi-Fi is available at most of the hotels, cafes and restaurants.

FURTHER READING

HISTORY

Probably the definitive book on Symi is 'Bus Stop Symi' by William Travis, published in 1970. The book documents the author's 3-year stay on Symi and gives a good account of life on the island at that time. It also gives a good background to the history of the island and the sponge-diving industry. Although currently out of print, second- hand copies can sometimes be found on Amazon.

'The Stone Wine Presses of Symi' by Sarantis Kritikos published in 1997 documents his discovery and rebuilding of some of the Byzantine wine presses on the Island. 'Moments of Silence' also by Sarantis Kritikos (2007) documents real stories from the lives of sponge divers. Sarantis is still resident on Symi and copies of his books can be found in some of the tourist shops in Yialos, including **Symi Souvenirs** just over the bridge next to the National bank. These are also available via kritikossarantis.com

LIVING ON SYMI

Adriana Shum has lived on Symi since 1993 and her regular blog documents life on the island through the seasons and provides useful insights for prospective visitors and those interested in following the latest events https://adrianashum.com/

James Collins is a resident accomplished author who has written a number of books on life on Symi including 'Carry on up the Kali Strata', 'Symi 85600' and 'Village View- A Year on Symi'. All of these are available on Amazon.

James has also written a screenplay for the film 'The Judas Inheritance', otherwise known as 'The Thirteenth', which was filmed on Symi. He also writes a regular blog about life on the island at http://www.symidream.com/

WALKING

Symi has many excellent walks and many people visit the island specifically for its hiking opportunities. A comprehensive hiking map (also the go-to map for Symi generally) has been produced by SKAÏ and Terrain Maps (http://www.terrainmaps.gr) and is available to buy either on the island or via Amazon. On the reverse of the map there is a list of trails with instructions.

A good website/blog for walks on Symi (and also other Greek islands) can be found at https://barrysramblings.com/greek-island-walks/ The site also has details of Barry Hankey's regular walks and research on the history and historic structures on the Island.

Lance Chilton's book entitled 'Walks in Symi' is unfortunately no longer available, although you may be lucky and find a second-hand copy.

TRAVEL

Andy Ward, who for many years supplied Symi Visitor Accommodation with travel information, now has his own travel blog at http://www.andyward.me.uk/symiblog/

This excellent blog is updated regularly with seasonal information on flights to Rhodes and Kos from many countries as well as information on ferries to Symi.

Symi also features on the excellent website 'Matt Barrett's Greece Guides', which is an excellent resource for travel planning throughout Greece. Consider booking hotels via Matt's links in order to keep the site adequately funded. Matt's page on all of the Dodecanese islands, including a good section on Symi, can be found at https://www.greektravel.com/greekislands/dodecanese.htm

PROPERTY FOR SALE & PROPERTY MAINTENANCE

For those interested in acquiring property on the island, there is a good choice of properties for sale by The Symi Estate Agent at http://thesymiestateagent.com/

For those that require advice or assistance in maintaining and servicing owned property, including holiday rentals on Symi, should contact Symi Property Services at http://symipropertyservices.com/

FEEDBACK & UPDATES

Inevitably things change and it is impossible to update a book such as this every time a change occurs. Restaurants, bars, hotels, and other establishments come and go, and new initiatives take hold. Ferry times can vary season to season as can the number of operators!

For more regular updates, and colour photographs of this wonderful island, please keep an eye on the accompanying 'Symi Practical Guide' facebook page, which can be found at @SymiPracticalGuide, and also the Instagram page of the same name.

Here you will find regular updates on everything to do with Symi. Please also leave feedback, both on the book itself, but also on any developments or changes on Symi that you feel can be incorporated into future editions. Happy Travels!

2024-1P

Printed in Great Britain
by Amazon